THE ROYAL SELANGOR STORY

To Vivian Dui Mei Chan
with all good wishes

from Mun Kuen

13/11/13

BORN AND BRED IN PEWTER DUST

THE ROYAL SELANGOR STORY

CHEN MAY YEE

ARCHIPELAGO PRESS

Copyright © Royal Selangor International Sdn Bhd 2003
Text © Chen May Yee 2003

Editor: Dianne Buerger, Lavinia Ng, Joane Sharmila
Design Consultant: Boon Lay Quistgaard
Designer: Lawrence Kok
Production Manager: Sin Kam Cheong

Royal Selangor International Sdn Bhd
4 Jalan Usahawan 6, Setapak Jaya
53300 Kuala Lumpur
Malaysia
Tel: (60) 3 4145 6000
Fax: (60) 3 4022 3000
www.royalselangor.com

First published in 2003 by ARCHIPELAGO PRESS
An imprint of Editions Didier Millet Sdn Bhd
25 Jalan Pudu Lama
50200 Kuala Lumpur
Malaysia
Tel: (60) 3 2031 3805
Fax: (60) 3 2031 6298
www.edmbooks.com

Reprinted 2007, 2012

Printed by Tien Wah Press Pte Ltd
Colour separation by Colourscan Co Pte Ltd
ISBN 978-981-4068-55-0

Pictures on pp. 2–8.

pp. 2–3: Chinese pewter tea caddy and antique hand tools from the Royal Selangor archives.

p. 4: The Ngeok Foh or Jade Peace touchmark, first used by Yong Koon.

p. 5: Antique pewter oil burner.

p. 8: Former employee Kian San, a master craftsman from China, polishing a cigarette box, 1965.

For my grandmother, Guay Soh Eng

CONTENTS

1115 - Pataling Street 510

PREFACE

More than a century ago, Yong Koon left his village in China with little more than his craftsman's tools and sailed to Malaysia – then known as Malaya – to start what would eventually become the largest pewter company in the world.

Like countless enterprises around Asia, the story begins with an old-fashioned patriarch and a tradition of skill and hard work. But then, the tale diverges from the norm. Unlike many other family concerns, this one has weathered two world wars, sibling feuds and the ongoing transformation of a cottage industry into a modern company. Royal Selangor started out making ceremonial vessels for the ancestral altars of overseas Chinese tin miners from pewter, a lustrous metal composed mainly of tin. Today, it produces an eclectic range of pewter creations that is sold in 26 countries and wins international design awards.

The company was named for the state of Selangor, where the Malaysian capital Kuala Lumpur is located. Its history is likewise entwined with Malaysia's as the country evolved from British colonial times to the modern era.

It was the tin in the muddy earth around Kuala Lumpur that brought my great-grandfather. A skilled pewtersmith, he joined his two brothers in the burgeoning mining town. Tin miners were their first customers, followed by British colonial officers and their wives. Much later, visitors bewitched by Malaysia's white beaches and rich culture stepped into the pewter shops, looking to take home a little piece of the country.

Petaling Street in Chinatown, Kuala Lumpur, 1800s.

That much can be explained by historical circumstance. But through the decades, the enterprise has sprouted wings. Though it is best known in Southeast Asia, its creations are also found in Harrods of London, Wako in Tokyo's Ginza district, and the design-oriented store Illums Bolighus in Copenhagen. It has commissioned designs from the likes of Erik Magnussen – the esteemed Danish designer – and its in-house Malaysian designers have collaborated with the Victoria and Albert Museum in London, drawing inspiration from the museum's vast collection of decorative art.

Along the way, Royal Selangor has acquired Seagull Pewter, Canada's biggest pewter maker, as well as Englefields, a 350-year-old London company that makes Crown & Rose pewter. It has diversified into fine jewellery, under the brand name Selberan, and into silver, with the acquisition of Comyns, the former London company of silversmiths with designs dating back to the 17th century.

Today, Royal Selangor remains in the hands of the founding Yong family. The patriarch's four grandchildren play active roles in the company, sharing responsibilities with a valued team of professional managers.

Sometimes, I like to imagine my great-grandfather walking into a modern-day Royal Selangor shop in, say, London. Peering through his wire-rimmed spectacles, he would see a collection of gleaming tea sets and candle stands, elegant cigar cases, vases and picture frames. And he would be astounded. Not at the exquisiteness of the creations, for they have always been exquisite, but at the transformation over the years of his little tinsmith shop.

I hope you enjoy reading this tale as much as I enjoyed writing it.

Chen May Yee, November 2003

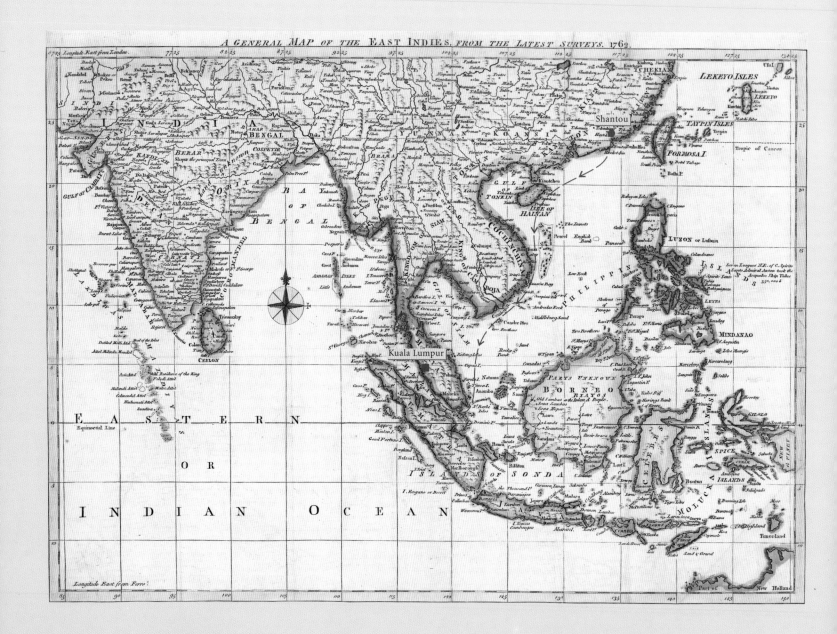

THE PEWTER PIONEERS

■ If it was gold that lured thousands of Chinese to California in the 19th century, it was tin that brought thousands of others to Malaysia.

Among them was a young pewtersmith named Yong Koon Seong. In 1885, he sailed from the southeastern Chinese port of Shantou in Guangdong province to Malaya, the British colonial name for the Malay peninsula. It wasn't a difficult decision to strike out; his village in Dabu, a remote enclave in Guangdong's hilly interior, offered neither fertile soil nor abundant business opportunities. Young people with ambition travelled north to the cities of Beijing or Shanghai, or east to Shantou where they boarded a ship heading across the South China Sea to Nanyang, as the Chinese called

Southeast Asia. The long-time travel restrictions imposed on Chinese citizens had just been eased and Chinese who ventured abroad were no longer regarded as traitors to the motherland.

They were drawn by new opportunities in Nanyang. British colonizers were consolidating power in Malaya, mostly with the acquiescence of the hereditary Malay rulers. As in other colonial outposts, mass immigration was a cornerstone of British rule. The British encouraged young Chinese men to travel to Malaya to work in the tin mines that were just being opened.

In those hard times, people grew up fast. At 11, Yong Koon Seong became an apprentice pewtersmith in the port town of Shantou, a major centre for Chinese pewter.

Mosque, Kuala Lumpur.

Jamek Mosque was built
in 1909 at the confluence of
the Klang and Gombak rivers.

Right: Yap Ah Loy, leader
of the Chinese community
in Kuala Lumpur from
1868 to 1885.

■ Kuala Lumpur means "muddy estuary" in Malay and it was a day's journey upriver from the more established port town of Klang. The small settlement was perched at the confluence of the Klang River and the Gombak River, where the waters were the colour of milky tea. A rough census in 1879 had put the town's population at 4,054.

At the time, it was a humble name for a humble place. The sky-scraping Petronas Twin Towers were still a century into the future and Kuala Lumpur in the late 19th century was little more than a ramshackle collection of mines, wooden huts, opium shops, gambling dens and brothels. All that was about to change. In 1880, five years before Yong Koon Seong arrived in Malaya, the British had moved the state capital from Klang to Kuala Lumpur, where the muddy river was rich in tin ore.

The British took over the administration of the area, until then controlled by Yap Ah Loy, a baby-faced but shrewd Hakka tin miner who was conferred the headman's

After three years learning his craft, Yong Koon Seong boarded a ship to Kuala Lumpur in 1885.

He joined an older brother, Chin Seong and a younger brother, Wai Seong, who had already established themselves as tinsmiths in the fledgling tin mining town.

The Hakkas

Yong Koon Seong, also known as Yong Koon, was a Hakka, one of the three main dialect groups of the Chinese who went overseas. (The two other major groups are the Cantonese and Hokkien.) In China, Hakkas are most often found in hilly regions on the periphery of more established societies.

More so than the Cantonese and Hokkiens, Hakkas have a history as sojourners. The name Hakka literally means "guest people". The Hakkas trace their roots to the Central Plains of northern China but moved southwards from the 14th century and soon could be found as minority populations across southern China. Because of their status as newcomers, Hakkas were often looked down upon by other less nomadic Chinese as a people without a homeland. Hakka women worked the fields and did not, as some of their Chinese sisters did to signify good breeding, bind their feet. For generations, Hakkas have regarded themselves and been regarded as outsiders; as a result, they have developed a stronger sense of community than the other dialect groups.

True to their Hakka wanderlust, Yong Koon and his brothers chose to spend the best part of their lives in a faraway country, eking a living in a frontier town that would evolve into modern Kuala Lumpur.

In his later years, Yong Koon often displayed another Hakka trait – a fierce pride in his heritage. If he caught a grandchild speaking a different Chinese dialect, he shouted grumpily: "Hakka people must speak Hakka! Otherwise you are a foreign devil!"

Yong Koon, 1920.

The outer wall and entrance to the Yong ancestral home in Pak Hou village, Dabu, 2001.

A cricket match in front of
the New Government offices,
c.1890s.

title of *Kapitan Cina*, or Chinese Captain, by
the Malay Muslim aristocracy.

It is impossible to know what Yong Koon
Seong thought of his new surroundings in
those days. He left neither diary nor letters.
For unknown reasons, he later shortened
his name to Yong Koon. What we do know
is that unlike some Chinese who went home
after earning a little bit of money, he
became part of the worldwide Chinese

diaspora, living the rest of his days in his
adopted country, Malaya.

Yong Koon's arrival in Kuala Lumpur in
1885 coincided with an era of frenzied construction. In 1886, a railway line from Kuala
Lumpur to Klang was completed, cutting the
journey from an entire day to just 43 minutes.
The railway made it possible to transport tin
from Kuala Lumpur to the port in Klang four
times a day. That same year saw the first

telegraph line in Kuala Lumpur. The first telephone lines were installed six years later.

On a hill across the river from the Chinese settlement, the British were building their government offices. Vegetable farms at the foot of the hill were uprooted to make a field for police parades. Beside that was the Selangor Club, with its black-and-white Tudor-style architecture and wide verandah from which the British could watch cricket matches on the parade ground, now known as Merdeka (Independence) Square.

Across the parade ground, the British erected a Moorish-style administration building in red brick with arches, minarets and courtyards, simply called the "New Government Offices." European tin mining companies and banks were busy setting up shop and in 1896, the town's first newspaper, the English-language Malay Mail, was printed. (The New Government Offices building was later renamed the "Federal Secretariat" and finally – after Malaya's independence in 1957 – the Sultan Abdul Samad Building, after the Sultan of Selangor at the time of its construction, 1897.)

The Land of Opportunity for Capitalist, Planter, Miner, Tourist.

BRITISH MALAYA is the largest individual exporter of TIN and the largest producer of Plantation RUBBER. Its other products include Copra, Coffee, Gambier, Tapioca and Spices. Few countries in the world have so much undeveloped natural wealth as the FEDERATED MALAY STATES.

Tin Exports in 1912, 48,420 tons value about £ 9,750,000.

Federated Malay States

Rubber Exports in 1912, 34,718,015 lbs., value about £ 7,500,000.

The FEDERATED MALAY STATES compare favourably with other Far Eastern tropical countries in regard to climate and cost of living, and there is a steady inflow of labour. With a Government which gives every encouragement to the development of progressive enterprises there is no better field for fresh capital than the FEDERATED MALAY STATES.

Full particulars about land, investments and industries supplied by the

MALAY STATES INFORMATION AGENCY, 88, CANNON STREET, LONDON, E.C.

An advertisement in 1913 by the Malay States Information Agency which campaigned heavily to attract people from all walks of life to British Malaya.

Yong Koon made pewter altarpieces for Chinese temples such as this one.

The wooden Chinese huts of Yap Ah Loy's time, linked by a maze of narrow passage-ways, were a fire menace. The British decreed that these be replaced by brick houses with terracotta tiled roofs. In these rows of two-storey shophouses, families traded down-stairs – the shop – in the day and slept upstairs – the house – at night.

It was in one of these shophouses located at No. 23, Cross Street, known today by its Malay name Jalan Silang, that Yong Koon and his brothers lived and worked. The shop was known as *Ngeok Foh* in Hakka or *Yu He* in Mandarin Pinyin. The name meant Jade Peace.

The Yong brothers were tinsmiths. They made a variety of simple household items for the town's fast-growing population – pails and gutters from galvanized steel as well as weighing scales used by merchants. Soon, the brothers began a side business making and selling pewter incense burners, joss stick holders and candle stands for the altars of Chinese prospectors, who were ever anxious to have the gods on their side. The Yong brothers employed a few crafts-men, who along with Yong Koon, were

By 1898, Malaya was the biggest producer of tin in the world, with an output of 40,000 tonnes per year. Besides Kuala Lumpur, there were also mining centres in Perak to the north and Negeri Sembilan and Melaka to the south. In Kuala Lumpur, the effects of the tin-mining boom transformed even the older parts of town.

Pewter in history

Pewter is made primarily from tin; the fourth most precious commercially traded metal after platinum, gold and silver. It is known as *zinn* in German, *étain* in French and *tenn* in Swedish. The use of pewter goes back to ancient times and the oldest piece of pewter on record is the pilgrim's bottle of Abydos in Egypt, which dates back to about 1500 BC. However, it was only around the 14th century that pewter became widely used at the Western dining table.

In 1348 AD, English pewterers set up a guild, which later decreed that every pewterer should "sett his marke" on each piece he produced. These touchmarks didn't just indicate the pewtersmith or company responsible for each object; they also vouched for the quality of the pieces. The guilds proliferated around Europe. For centuries, Europeans ate off pewter bowls and plates and drank from pewter tankards until the use of china tableware became fashionable.

In Asia, pewter was first used in China, more than 2,000 years ago. Asia has the richest tin mining belt in the world, which runs from Yunan and Guangdong in southern China through Laos, Burma, Thailand, Peninsular Malaysia and Singapore to Indonesia. Unlike in the West though, Chinese pewter was mainly for ceremonial purposes and not the dining table, where chinaware had long been preferred. Chinese immigrants brought the craft of pewter-making to parts of Southeast Asia.

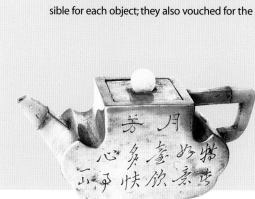

Left: An antique pewter piece from China.

From top right: A Chinese wine ewer; an English tankard; and a colonial American coffeepot, all antique pewter pieces from the Royal Selangor archival collection.

Opposite: A studio portrait in 1920 of Yong Koon with sons, left to right: Peng Pow, Peng Kai and Peng Sin.

Yong Koon's first shop was at No. 23, Cross Street, known today by its Malay name, Jalan Silang.

among Kuala Lumpur's first pewtersmiths. Just as silver pieces have hallmarks, pewter pieces have touchmarks. The Yong brothers' touchmark, *Ngeok Foh*, was stamped in Chinese characters on each piece of pewter produced.

■ By the 1920s, there were five rival shops on bustling Cross Street. All were involved in tinsmithing, fashioning weighing scales and crafting pewter and each was owned by a family bearing the Yong surname. At *Ngeok Foh*, three pewtersmiths worked in the front of the shophouse. Parents planning their children's weddings came to order altarpieces, teapots and wine ewers, or sent match-makers to make the purchases. The more cost-conscious customers brought with them old pewter pieces to be remelted; the melted tin would go towards the new purchase, and the customer would be credited for the material when the final price was tallied.

Like many young Chinese men of his time, Yong Koon went back to China to find a wife. Her name was Loh Pat. Soon after the marriage, Yong Koon returned alone to Malaya. It was seven years before Yong Koon made another trip home, to see his first-born son Peng Pow for the first time and to bring his wife and son to Malaya. In Kuala Lumpur, three more sons – Peng Sin, Peng Kai and Peng Seong – were born in quick succession. The family continued to live at the *Ngeok Foh* shophouse, in the Chinese

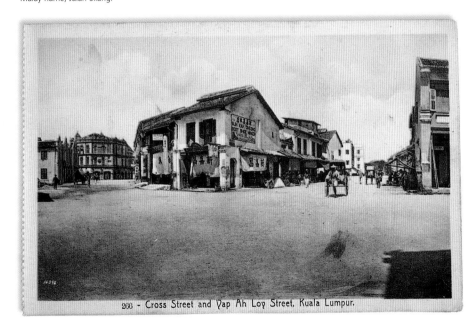

266 - Cross Street and Yap Ah Loy Street, Kuala Lumpur.

extended family way. Peng Kai later said they were "born and bred in pewter dust."

As is so often the case, it is the patriarch who is remembered and credited for his descendants' success. Yet Yong Koon would probably not have gone far without his formidable wife, Loh Pat, by his side. She was a no-nonsense Hakka woman whose business acumen exceeded that of her husband. Those who remember say Yong Koon was fonder of drinking and betting on horse races than he was of hard work. Loh Pat was the industrious one.

■ Along with tin, rubber was becoming a big export commodity for Malaya. Thousands of acres of virgin rainforest were cleared and tidy rows of rubber trees planted in its place. Loh Pat saw an opportunity, and began making thousands of small zinc spouts and selling them to rubber plantations. These spouts were attached to the trunks of rubber trees, to funnel the milky-white latex dribbling from cuts on the tree bark into a waiting cup. From the money she saved, Loh Pat bought gold rings – one at a time – which she strung around her waist under her tunic for safekeeping.

Yong Koon (with hand on child's shoulder) in front of his shop in Cross Street, Kuala Lumpur, 1911.
The child holding the hat is Peng Pow, Yong Koon's oldest son.

The woman in white looking out of the upstairs window is Loh Pat, Yong Koon's wife.

In 1930, the gold rings bought Yong Koon's family their own shophouse at No. 219, Pudu Road, at the edge of town in an area best described by its Chinese name "half jungle." The shophouse was no palace, but it was their own. Located next to a fruit orchard and Pudu Prison, the shophouse had a terracotta-tiled roof and a front entrance with cowboy-style swinging doors, known as *pintu pagar*. Upstairs, louvred French windows were opened to let shafts of sunlight into the family's living area. At night, horizontal wooden bars were pulled across the front door for security.

Eldest son Peng Pow, then 25, ran the first primitive pewter factory. His brothers pitched in after school, even the youngest, Peng Seong, who was only seven at the time. The company was called Malayan Pewter Works.

It was the 1930s and Malaya felt the world depression as keenly as anywhere else did. For the little family of pewtersmiths, life was doubly tough: not only was it hard to find customers, it was hard to find workers. The profession was regarded as a dying craft from the old country and many pewtersmiths had switched to other jobs such as sewing clothes.

To find workers, Loh Pat travelled around the peninsula, tapping into the equivalent of today's internet recruitment websites – the Yong clan network, the Hakka network and the Dabu village network.

To bump up sales, Loh Pat and her third son Peng Kai, who was barely out of his teens, organized the first pewter exhibition at the Chamber of Mines in the northern Malayan tin mining town of Ipoh. They approached rich Chinese tin miners who were hurting from a slump in world tin prices, and tried to persuade them of the virtuous cycle that would be created if pewter sales took off. They suggested that each miner buy a few pewter items each, which would give Malayan Pewter Works the capital to expand its business, which presumably would mean more demand for the tin produced by the miners.

"We asked each one to order a few pieces, each one adding up to about 50 dollars. If ten of them [buy], it is 500 dollars! You see?" Peng Kai explained many decades later. "At least they can say, this is something new." Unfortunately, there is no record of whether that marketing tactic succeeded.

An antique incense burner altarpiece, 1930.

On a business trip to Kedah state in northern Malaya in 1936, according to her grandson, Yong Poh Seong, Loh Pat was bitten on the leg by a mosquito. The bite festered, and she fell ill and died, aged 56.

The only surviving photograph of Loh Pat shows her as a young bride just arrived in Malaya (see p. 24). Her hair is pulled back, exposing a high forehead and heavy earrings. She is half-smiling. She and another woman are looking at the camera from the upstairs window of the shophouse on Cross Street, separate from the men posing with their hats and their pipes in front of the shop downstairs.

■ At Pudu Road, Yong Koon, now in his 60s, handled the accounts and kept track of the ten employees, marking attendance as they showed up for work each day. Every evening before dinner, he hailed a rickshaw, pulled by a man on foot, which took him to a bar down the street. There, he ordered a *stengah*, a half shot of whiskey, which was served with a bowl of peanuts. How many stengahs he consumed depended on how much money he had in his pocket, remembers his grandson Yong Poh Seong, who

Loh Pat,
1911.

Opposite: Yong Koon at
Dusun Tua hot springs,
Selangor, 1937.

accompanied his grandfather on these trips as a young boy.

In fact, pewter sales were sluggish in those days so Yong Koon could not have had too many opportunities to get tipsy. The Chinese in Malaya were ordering fewer ceremonial items. Like immigrant groups everywhere, they were simply observing fewer ceremonies. Slowly, other traditional pewtersmiths in Malaya were going out of business.

The family was faced with the prospect of being part of a sunset industry. It was around this time that the company's products and clientele began to change. An English engineer, G.H. Hutton, who worked with Anglo Oriental Ltd., a British tin mining company in Malaya, suggested that the Yong family take advantage of the low price of tin at the time to make more utilitarian items. The engineer didn't just offer advice; he made a loan of 500 Malayan dollars as working capital. And so, Malayan Pewter began making European-style cigarette boxes, ashtrays, vases and teapots for British and other Western expatriates. It was an important change in direction, laying the foundation for an export market in the future.

Business picked up and the crisis passed. When Peng Sin got married, Peng Pow gave him 360 Malayan dollars for wedding expenses including the making of a new suit. Peng Kai enjoyed the same largesse when he married, and chose to spend part of his marriage allowance on a Dunlop mattress, then an almost unheard-of luxury.

But the good times were brief. Tensions were already building in the crowded confines of the shophouse on Pudu Road. And the Second World War was approaching. ☐

In order to survive, the Yongs began to make pewter pieces that appealed to expatriates, including cigarettete boxes.

This piece from the Royal Selangor archival collection features a motif of the Sultan Abdul Samad Building. The Selangor Pewter name is written in Japanese characters.

The old Chinese way of making pewter

A pewtersmith, usually an older man from the Hakka community, began by melting the metal in a wok over a charcoal fire. Tin is a soft metal and in the early days, lead and antimony were added to harden it. Another reason to add lead was that it was cheaper than tin. Ceremonial items often had as much as 20 per cent lead content while tableware had about ten per cent. (Today, all Royal Selangor table and drinkware is lead-free.)

Once the metal had been heated to the right temperature, as gauged by the pewtersmith, it was ladled and poured slowly between two terracotta tiles to cast a pewter sheet. The tiles were mounted flat on a wooden base and tilted slightly backwards to allow the metal to flow in. Paper strips were wedged along three sides of the tiles, with the topmost edge left open to receive the metal. The thicker the paper strips along the edges, the thicker the cast pewter sheet.

The casting procedure required an experienced eye, a steady hand…and strong thighs. The pewtersmith squatted on top of the tiles and leaned backward as he poured the liquid metal into the top opening. When he finished pouring, he leaned forward again, his weight against the tiles squeezing excess metal out into a bamboo receptacle placed just under the opening. This excess metal was later remelted for the next sheet.

The cast sheet, measuring 12 or 16 inches square, was cooled and scraped with a steel blade to remove a layer of oxide. Then, somewhat as a tailor cut patterns from a piece of fabric, a pewtersmith cut patterns from the pewter sheet. The body of a plain teapot, for example, would be cut as a rectangle, wrapped around a cylindrical wooden "chuck," and knocked into shape with a wooden mallet. The pewter cylinder was soldered along the edges, and the rough edges filed. Other parts of the teapot, such as the bottom, were also cut from the pewter sheet and soldered on in the same manner. These simple methods were used to create some almost impossibly delicate designs, such as the famous melon-shaped teapot, which has a body made up of 12 segments and is one of the finest surviving examples of Ngeok Foh pewter.

Spouts and handles were usually cast in greenstone moulds. These were slabs of greenstone with cavities carved into them. Again, it took an experienced pewtersmith to cast a spout. He poured molten pewter into a mould at just the right temperature so that an outer skin cooled and hardened; yet the molten metal inside remained hot enough to flow out, forming a hollow spout. The spout was then soldered onto the body of the teapot.

The completed item was filed to remove rough edges and polished with a rough leaf known by its scientific name Tetracera scandens or simply "stone leaf". The upper part of the tropical leaf is covered with tiny barbs and was used as a sandpaper substitute in the old days.

A single pewtersmith saw the entire job through from the casting to polishing.

Pewtersmiths often specialized: there were candle stand experts, teapot experts, and so on.

In China, individual pewtersmiths plied their trade from door to door, carrying benches, tiles and assorted files and hammers with them. Working in a customer's home was a way of assuring suspicious clients that the pewter alloy was not adulterated with cheaper metals. In Malaysia though, the pewtersmiths tended to base themselves in tinsmith shops such as Ngeok Foh.

Right: Traditional tools and greenstone moulds.

Left: *Tetracera scandens* or "stone leaf". The fine sandpaper-like leaf of this plant was used by early manufacturers of pewter to hand-polish their products.

Following page: Yong Koon's hand tools.

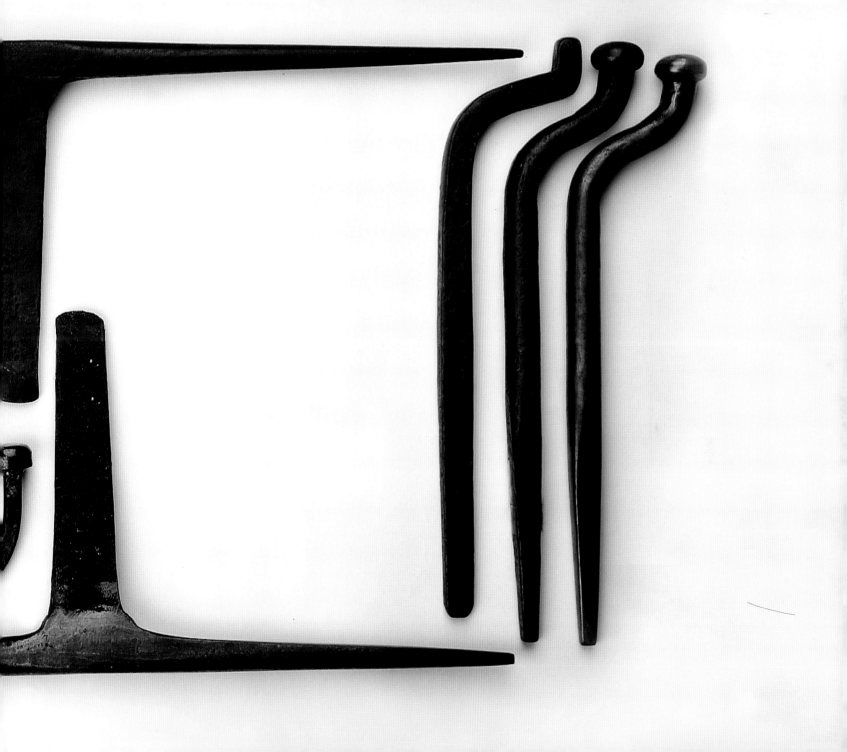

WORLD WAR AND FAMILY FEUDS

A pewter figurine of a policeman, 1950s.

Opposite: Malayan Army Transport drivers performing a drill before the Second World War.

■ The four brothers squabbled over how best to run the business. As in so many family disputes, the issues involved the head as well as the heart. As the brothers shuffled allegiances, the next decade would see the formation of three other pewter companies – Tiger Pewter, Selangor Pewter and Lion Pewter. Only one, Selangor Pewter, later renamed Royal Selangor, survives.

In 1938, eldest brother Peng Pow left Pudu Road under unhappy circumstances.

According to Peng Pow's son, Poh Seong, his father's departure stemmed from a simple misunderstanding. Peng Pow wanted to move his young family to a place of their own and the three other brothers mistook that as a sign that they were being abandoned. "The three started a revolution," and recruited their elderly father Yong Koon to their side, Poh Seong told the author, adding that the younger brothers demanded that Peng Pow leave behind "machinery and cash".

Third brother Peng Kai had a different take on the family feud. Under Peng Pow, the pewter objects were still made the old-fashioned way. An experienced pewtersmith saw the process through from beginning to end, casting a pewter sheet, shaping, soldering and filing the item, and polishing the finished product. Each pewtersmith pro-tected his turf fiercely, there was no division of labour and the process was slow. "The skilled workers did not allow younger people to learn," Peng Kai later complained. It was Peng Pow's reluctance to modernize the process that led to the split between him and the three younger brothers, Peng Kai said.

Traditional large pewter teapot, 1900s.

Company stationery from
the various companies
run by the brothers.

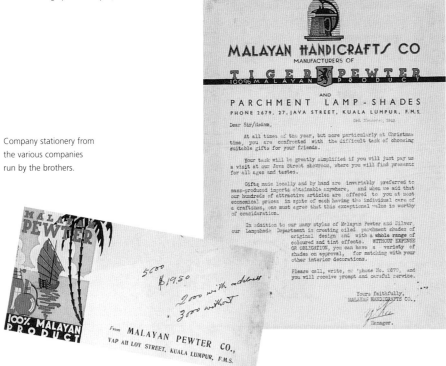

What is certain is that Peng Pow moved away. He continued manufacturing pewter using the business name of Malayan Pewter. The others remained at Pudu Road and in 1940, started a rival company, Tiger Pewter, with a couple of workers.

But with very little capital and no distribution network, Tiger Pewter folded within a year. In 1942, they tried again, starting Selangor Pewter. This time though, pewter wasn't the only thing they produced. Peng Sin and Peng Kai turned to a hodge-podge of jobs to make ends meet, mostly opportunistic, under the umbrella name Malayan Handicrafts. The youngest brother, Peng Seong, helped out after school.

Yellowed sheets of stationery from that time give us an idea of the many businesses the brothers dabbled in. Under the letter-head "Malayan Handicrafts Co." are the words "Manufacturers of Malayan Pewter, Malayan Silver, Malayan Pottery, Parchment Lamp-Shades, Wooden Toys, A.R.P. Equipment & Victory Badges". The address is 27, Java Street. (Java Street has since been renamed twice, to Mountbatten Road and later, Jalan Tun Perak.)

■ It was a time of great uncertainty. "Nobody was buying pewter! War was going to start. The Japanese were coming nearer," Peng Sin said in a 1982 interview.

So Peng Sin and Peng Kai began making Air Raid Precaution (A.R.P.) tin lamp covers to camouflage populated areas from Japanese bomber planes at night. They also

The melon pot

One of the most stunning pieces to survive intact from Yong Koon's early years in Malaya is a melon-shaped teapot. With a stout segmented body and a whimsical stem on the lid, it bears the *Ngeok Foh* touchmark. The pot is notable for its intricacy: each of the 12 segments that make up the body was individually cut from a pewter sheet and carefully hammered into shape in the old way, then soldered together. Such antique pieces are rare. In the past, families often had their old pewter pieces melted down, so the tin could go towards making new items for a son or daughter's wedding.

How this melon pot made its way full circle back into the hands of the Yong family is a saga in itself.

It was the Second World War and the Japanese were advancing into Malaya from the north. As the British retreated southwards along the peninsula, they dropped bombs to destroy supplies that the advancing Japanese army might find useful.

But for hungry villagers in Kajang, a small village south of Kuala Lumpur, the gnawing in their bellies proved stronger than the fear of being blown up. Even as bombs rained down, desperate people scrambled into a well-stocked warehouse to grab bags of rice to feed their families.

Like everyone else, a young man known only as Ah Ham ran in to get food. Unlike the others, he emerged with a piece of history. Amid the mayhem in the warehouse, the villager spied a melon-shaped teapot. As he bent to pick it up, he heard shrapnel whiz just above his head. A shaking Ah Ham ran out clutching the pot, convinced the vessel must have mystical powers that saved his life.

For decades afterwards, Ah Ham entertained friends with his wartime story as he poured them tea from the melon pot. One of these friends happened to be Chen Shoo Sang, who had married a granddaughter of Yong Koon. When Ah Ham asked his friend to take the melon pot to the pewter factory for a polish, someone immediately recognised the *Ngeok Foh* touchmark and persuaded Ah Ham to part with it for a small sum of money.

The melon pot is now in the company's archival collection. It has spawned a line of reproduction melon-shaped teapots and tea caddies.

Ah Ham's lucky melon-shaped teapot now resides in Royal Selangor's archival collection.

made A.R.P. water pumps – consisting of a bucket, a long hose and a hand pump – for putting out fires ignited by bombs.

The British tried to defend Malaya against the approaching Japanese. But they miscalculated badly. The British stationed most of their troops and their cannons off the southern tip of Malaya in Singapore, in anticipation of a sea assault. On 8 December, 1941, Japanese soldiers attacked instead from the north, landing on the shores of northern Malaya and southern Thailand. Mocking the formidable British military hardware amassed in Singapore, the Japanese cycled in on simple bicycles through rubber plantations. By 15 February the following year, the Japanese had sunk British warships and taken over Singapore.

The brothers' pewter business crumbled. The European expatriates who had been their core clientele fled. Those still in Malaya were living under vastly altered circumstances, as internees. Because of Japan's war with China, the Chinese community in Malaya suffered disproportionately. Down the road from the Pudu factory, in front of the Pavilion Cinema, the heads of those who defied the Japanese were mounted on stakes as an example to others.

The Japanese declared tin a controlled commodity. They limited the Yong brothers to making sake sets as gifts for Japanese military officials, ensuring a small supply of tin specifically for that purpose. Each sake set comprised two sake bottles and three or five little cups, and was presented in a velvet-lined

Japanese army soldiers cycle into Malaya on 8 December, 1941.

varnished wood box with a sliding cover. The factory was required to keep detailed records of the tin used, since it was considered a strategic material in times of war. Failure to keep records was a serious offence carrying the threat of severe punishment.

The sake sets were hardly enough to put food on the table. To supplement his family's income, Peng Kai briefly ran a taxi service. Since there was no petrol to be had, he drove a converted old car with a charcoal burner at the back. Every now and then, he'd have to stop the car and feed in more charcoal. To attract customers, he stood at the market and shouted destinations: "Seremban! Mantin! Kajang!"

■ Some time during the war, eldest brother Peng Pow was kidnapped and killed by gangsters from one of the secret societies that made up the Chinese underground. In 1945, the war over, the British returned in the form of the British Military Administration. The Yong brothers, minus Peng Pow, were again re-positioning themselves.

Second brother Peng Sin branched off on his own, taking over an old leather shop on Batu Road, the town's main commercial street. The most artistically inclined of the brothers, Peng Sin had been an avid reader of London's Studio magazine and the Art Deco influences of the time can be seen in his designs for signboards and posters for the successive pewter companies. At Batu Road, he fashioned some items under the name Lion Pewter for a brief period. In 1947, his wife, Lim Choon Neo, died. Unable to cope with running a household of four children in addition to a factory of 20 workers, Peng Sin gave up the pewter trade.

"I couldn't stand it anymore," he said later. "I preferred to have a good rest." He got married again within months to Chan Yoke Hup. For the rest of his working life, he made cane furniture and parchment lampshades, mostly for the homes of European expatriates. Peng Sin also painted. As chairman of the Selangor Art Society, he knew famed Malaysian artist Yong Mun Sen

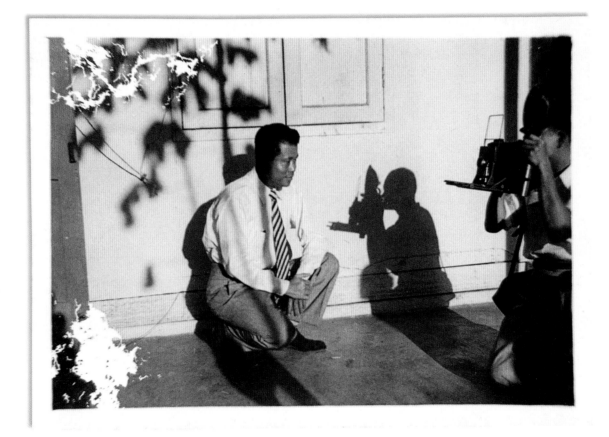

The portrait of Yong Koon by Malaysian artist Yong Mun Sen.

(no direct relation), whom he persuaded to paint his aged father, Yong Koon. Yong Koon posed for the oil painting in a white cotton vest. The brown suit and dark tie he wears in the finished portrait, which hangs today at the company's headquarters in Kuala Lumpur, is from the artist's imagination.

Third brother Peng Kai and fourth brother Peng Seong, now out of school, continued to run Selangor Pewter out of Pudu Road. Just after the war, Peng Pow's widow approached them for help, asking if they would merge Selangor Pewter with the ailing Malayan Pewter. Peng Seong agreed, Peng Kai didn't. As a compromise, the two brothers jointly ran the two companies as separate entities for a few months. Before long, the brothers parted ways, with Peng Seong taking over Malayan Pewter and Peng Kai continuing with his Selangor Pewter.

■ In those immediate post-war years, the pewter business was so precarious that Peng Kai accepted cigarettes from the British forces as payment for his tankards, ashtrays and cigarette boxes. He then sold the cigarettes on the black market for cash.

In this way, Selangor Pewter scraped by. Malayan Pewter didn't, sputtering to an end in 1950. Peng Seong joined The Straits Times, an English-language broadsheet, as a photographer, and went on to set up Yong Peng Seong Studio, supplying news photographs to the likes of the Associated Press and the now-defunct Singapore Standard newspaper. Peng Seong became so well-known as a photographer that he travelled with Tunku Abdul Rahman (who would become Malaysia's first prime minister), to London to document the negotiations leading to the colony's independence in 1957.

By 1950, Peng Kai was the only brother still in the pewter trade. As he put it to an interviewer when he was in his 70s, his voice wistful: "I became alone." □

Opposite: Peng Seong, the photographer in the family, taking a photo of Peng Kai.

Malayan pewter

MALAYAN PEWTER Co
OPPOSITE THE FEDERAL DISPENSARY

YOUNG

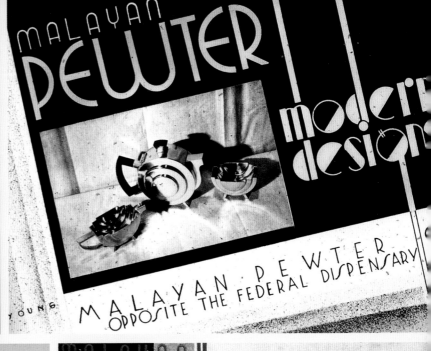

MALAYAN PEWTER

modern designs

MALAYAN PEWTER
OPPOSITE THE FEDERAL DISPENSARY

YOUNG

This Christmas give MALAYAN PEWTER

MALAYAN PEWTER Co
YAP AH LOY STREET
KUALA LUMPUR

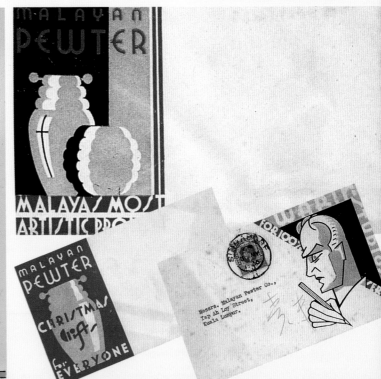

MALAYAN PEWTER

MALAYA'S MOST ARTISTIC PRO...

MALAYAN PEWTER
CHRISTMAS gifts for EVERYONE

FOR 100...

Messrs. Malayan Pewter Co.,
Yap Ah Loy Street,
Kuala Lumpur.

malayan pewter

Peng Sin used his artistic talents to create many of the promotional materials used in the brothers' various companies. Colourful hand-dyed glass plates with an Art Deco influence were used as advertising slides in the cinema. The Art Deco influence can also be seen in the catalogues and stationery produced at the time.

1947—PRICE LIST

GIFTS FOR ALL OCCASIONS

100% MALAYAN PRODUCT

275 Tea and Coffee Set   276 Tea and Coffee Set   272 Tea-Set   273 Tea and Coffee Set

A FRESH START:

SELANGOR PEWTER

■ Well, Peng Kai wasn't quite alone. In 1938, he had married Guay Soh Eng, a young Hokkien woman whose parents owned a bicycle repair shop in Kuala Lumpur. Soh Eng and Peng Kai met through friends and by all accounts, it was a love match.

Unlike many Chinese girls of her generation, who were often kept in seclusion at home until it was time for them to marry, Soh Eng was educated by Catholic nuns at the Convent Bukit Nanas (Pineapple Hill Convent), until she turned 12. Later, at her family's bicycle repair shop, she was often found with her sleeves rolled up, patching a punctured tyre or straightening a greasy bicycle chain.

By the end of the war in 1945, the couple had four small children to feed. Peace may have arrived but the business continued to languish. They figured that if the pewter company were to survive, they needed direct access to customers. People could hardly be expected to traipse over to the Pudu Road factory, with its clattering machines and hot cauldrons of molten pewter.

But Peng Kai and Soh Eng didn't have the money to rent a shop. So they rented half a shop, on Kuala Lumpur's busiest shopping street, Batu Road. (The street is now known as Jalan Tuanku Abdul Rahman, named after Malaysia's first king.) Already, the street was a lively mix of the

Peng Kai and Soh Eng's wedding party at the Kam Leng Garden Cafe, Kuala Lumpur, 1938.

Peng Kai in the family home (which doubled as an office) above the factory, 1950s.

migrant cultures that would later make up part of independent Malaysia.

Selangor Pewter shared its premises with China Arts, which imported embroidered linen and lacquer ware, mostly for the wives of British army officers. Their neighbours included some of the town's fanciest retailers, some of which are still there today. Across the street was G.S. Gill, a sports equipment store run by a family of Sikhs. They ordered pewter trophies from Selangor Pewter. At the end of the street was P.H. Hendry, the royal jeweller. Mr Hendry was a

Peng Kai and Soh Eng in the early days, in front of the Pudu Road factory.

Sri Lankan Buddhist who started out in 1902 with a small jewellery showcase in his father's bakery. By the late 1940s, he had his own shop and three royal warrants from three different Malay sultans. He crafted medals and regalia for the sultans and sold fine English silver for their palaces.

Also on Batu Road, the Chinese-run Canton Tailor and Fook Tailor custom-made Western-style suits. Around the corner, on Mountbatten Road (now Jalan Tun Perak), were Kuala Lumpur's two premier department stores – Robinson's and Whiteaway, Laidlaw and Co. Ltd. At the other end of Batu Road, the family-run Lee Wong Kee restaurant served up sumptuous Chinese banquets next to the landmark Odeon Cinema.

■ At the Batu Road shop, Soh Eng sold the pewter vases, pitchers, ashtrays and cigarette boxes that Peng Kai made in his Pudu Road factory. It was a one-woman operation; she served customers, swept the floor, dusted the glass shelves, and kept the books. At the back of the shop was a big wooden desk, where one or two of her children could be found most days, head bent over homework.

"Malaya's Finest Gift" was made at the factory on Pudu Road, 1950s.

Peng Kai was the proud owner of a 350 cc Norton motorbike, which he used for deliveries.

45

No. 219 Pudu Road. Bought by Loh Pat in 1930, the factory was on the ground floor of this shophouse with its Coca-Cola sign.

Peng Kai had taught Soh Eng to drive, placing a cup of water on the dashboard which she wasn't allowed to spill as she drove, presumably to discourage the twin sins of jerkiness and high speed. In those days, a woman behind the wheel was nothing short of revolutionary. When Soh Eng drove a green Austin van around town delivering pewter, she attracted shouts and stares from small children, who would point at the vivacious driver wearing a *samfu*, the floral Chinese pantsuit.

Peng Kai and Soh Eng's children grew up in an environment where family intertwined with business. Poh Shin, a son, was born in 1939, daughter Mun Ha in 1941, daughter Mun Kuen in 1942, and son Poh Kon in 1945.

They lived above the factory, up the worn wooden stairs past the ancestral altar, where Soh Eng lit joss sticks everyday in front of black-and-white photos of her late father and mother-in-law. In the day, the incessant rumble of the polishing machines came through the floorboards from downstairs.

Money was still scarce and there were few frills. In the evenings, each child slept on a rattan mat rolled out on the floor, with a pillow, blanket and bolster. They bathed standing up in the middle of the upstairs kitchen, scooping cold water out of a big tin pail. If someone was cooking, the bather had to wait.

The children attended English school, the boys at Methodist Boys' School and the girls at Pudu English School. The children excelled academically and were popular. Three were appointed school prefects, while two made it to the level of school captain. Peng Kai himself had a bilingual education, having first attended the Chinese-medium Confucian School followed by English language study at the Methodist Boys' School. He was convinced that having an English education was crucial for succeeding in business. Under the British, all official correspondence was in English. English was also needed for writing to expatriate customers who had returned home, to keep them up to date on new designs and promotions.

After school, his children took telephone orders, packed pewter and painted labels on boxes. Growing up with the business left an indelible stamp on the children – they learned about hard work, thrift, and family duty and commitment. On one of the children, the mark was physical.

One day, Peng Kai was wielding a blowtorch in his factory when a gust of wind blew the flame towards his first-born son, Poh Shin. The boy, aged four, suffered terrible burns on his legs. It was during the Japanese occupation and shortages meant that there were no painkillers available. The boy lay in bed for a year. His father was wracked with guilt at the pain caused to his son. When the boy was well enough to learn to walk again, Peng Kai took him cycling everyday to strengthen his legs.

■ In Soh Eng, Peng Kai had found not just an equal partner in life and work, but also a much needed counterbalance to his own workaholic character. While Soh Eng worked hard, she also had a great sense of fun. Some evenings in the Pudu factory, she and her cousins cleared away the worktables and invited a dance instructor to teach them the Western dances of the time, such as the rumba, the cha-cha and the swing.

By contrast, Peng Kai had few friends and no hobbies. When he read, it was magazines

The Yong family, 1957.
Front row, left to right:
Mun Ha, Soh Eng,
Peng Kai and Mun Kuen.
Back row, left to right:
Poh Kon and Poh Shin.

such as Popular Mechanics, from which he gleaned new ideas for mechanizing some of the more laborious processes in making pewter. When he took his family to the beach on weekends, he also took along his employees, jammed shoulder to shoulder on two makeshift wooden benches he had installed in the back of his van.

When business was bad, Peng Kai fretted that he wouldn't be able to feed his four children. When business was booming, he wished he had more children to help him. Worrying late into the night, he sometimes looked at his sleeping wife in exasperation, shook her awake and demanded to know how on earth she could sleep when they had so many problems.

Peng Kai used to say, "My wife is my right arm," according to his great friend and confidante, Sun Sai Lum, a retired police officer who now lives in Singapore. "She was the stabilising factor, very calm and very level-headed," says Sai Lum. "He was the highly-stressed worrier."

■ In 1952, the patriarch Yong Koon died, aged 81. With his death ended the era of

Poh Shin, Poh Kon and Peng Kai experimenting with machinery, 1961.

Yongs who had been born in China. His older brother, Yong Chin Seong, had also died in Malaya. Chin Seong's descendants continued to work as tinsmiths in Kuala Lumpur until falling demand for weighing scales – their bread and butter – finally caused *Ngeok Foh* to close sometime after the Second World War.

The younger brother, Yong Wai Seong, returned to China sometime during or before the 1930s, to the Yong ancestral home. This branch of the family remains in the farming village of Pak Hou in Dabu, Guangdong province.

Opposite: Peng Kai and Soh Eng (centre) with their children, employees, and relatives, 1957.

Mun Kuen checking engraved items before despatch to customers. 1959.

The Proclamation of Independence was signed by Malaya's prime minister, Tunku Abdul Rahman, on 31st August 1957. A limited edition plate was made in 1977 to commemorate the 20th anniversary of Malaysian independence.

For Yong Koon's sons however, there was no longer the question of whether to return to the ancestral village. They wrote regularly to their relatives in Dabu, sending money to help fix a leaking roof or to buy a tub of precious lard for cooking. But they were Malayan, born and bred. They had put down roots in their father's adopted land.

In 1957, Malaya achieved independence. Unlike in some other colonies, the handover of power was negotiated without bloodshed. Tunku Abdul Rahman, a Cambridge-educated Malay prince, became prime minister. He headed a coalition led by the United Malays National Organisation and made up of other race-based parties representing the more recent immigrant groups – the Chinese and the Indians.

The name change to Malaysia came later, in 1963, with the addition of the states of Sabah and Sarawak in North Borneo as well as Singapore. The Malaysia-Singapore relationship, however, was a turbulent one, and the Malay-led Malaysian government and the Chinese-led Singaporean leadership parted ways in 1965.

■ At Pudu Road, Selangor Pewter began to grow. Unlike Peng Pow's Malayan Pewter, which was full of crotchety old craftsmen working at a leisurely pace, at Selangor Pewter, Peng Kai introduced a semblance of a production line. He had no patience with egos. Prospective workers were told straight out they had to be game for anything, whether it was polishing pewter or sweeping floors.

In Peng Kai's factory, young men in white vests and baggy shorts cast the pewter sheets out by the big back door. If they were lucky, a breeze blew in to cool the air around the bubbling cauldrons of molten pewter. Even before 1950, the company was no longer casting flat pewter sheets between two

The ones who stayed behind

Yong Koon's ancestral home doesn't appear to have changed much since he left in the 1880s, nor does the farming village of Pak Hou. Pak Hou means "One Hundred Noblemen", for the numerous scholars it produced. It is a village in Dabu, in Guangdong province.

Yong Wai Seong was the only one in Yong Koon's generation to return to China. Today, his widowed daughter-in-law, Wong Nyet Ngoh, tends the walled family compound, with its cobblestone passages linking some 40 rooms. She has lived in the Yong compound since 1937, when she arrived in Pak Hou from the port town of Shantou as the 16-year-old bride of Wai Seong's son, Peng Nam.

Many of the rooms are empty today. Following in the footsteps of generations before them, young people such as Nyet Ngoh's son have moved on to better prospects elsewhere, in the booming economic zones that are the new face of China. Some rooms are barricaded.

Others contain a few dusty family relics that survived the Cultural Revolution: a large brown earthen jar, stacked porcelain teacups, cobwebbed baskets. The family kitchen, with its giant wok and sooty chimney, is hardly used these days. There is a well for water, pigs in pens and shrivelled vegetables drying on the roof.

The once-grand Yong clan hall has collapsed in places, opening it to the sky. These days, there are no weddings or clan celebrations there, just chickens and geese pecking amongst tall piles of straw. A large sign on a wall translates roughly as "Hall of Plentiful Grain".

Outside the curving walls of the family compound, there are rice fields, vegetable gardens and a wide river. Turn left on the dusty unpaved road and it leads you to the town centre, with its dilapidated rows of shops and stalls. Amongst the dust and peeling paint, a prominent new school building erected by overseas Chinese stands out in all its white-tiled glory. Turn right and the road

takes you to a local government office, where Nyet Ngoh's granddaughter works. A sign by the gate lists in detail the rules and penalties of China's One Child Policy.

Back in the Yong compound, there are several reminders of the parallel branch of the family in Nanyang: a pile of yellowed letters with Malaysian stamps on the envelopes and faded photographs. There is a stout metal basin in which the old lady once bathed her babies and a pewter wine ewer with a small phoenix motif, brought back from Malaya some 70 years ago. Nyet Ngoh's son, Fook Seong, an administrative worker in Shenzhen, says he has invited his mother to move in with his family, but she won't leave the ancestral home.

Wong Nyet Ngoh, who married into the Yong family, still lives in the ancestral home which contains a few pewter heirlooms.

Opposite: Mun Ha
at the Selangor Pewter
half-shop at 219 Batu Road,
Kuala Lumpur, 1960.

Peng Kai discussing the finer
points of his product with
Malaysia's first prime minister,
Tunku Abdul Rahman, 1958.

terracotta tiles in the old Chinese way. Peng Kai devised an updated version made of iron slabs held together with hinges, between which the liquid metal was poured to cool and harden into a pewter sheet.

He also introduced a spinning lathe, which sped up the process of forming objects from the flat pewter sheets. Instead of fashioning the cut sheets with a wooden mallet over a stationary wooden chuck to shape objects, the chuck was spun with a motor. An expert then applied or eased

pressure on the rotating pewter sheet with a steel forming device to shape the object.

Towards the front of the building, young women wearing *samfu* and wooden clogs sat in rows, polishing pewter. A single belt attached to an electric motor operated about 10 machines; the machines spun the pewter objects as the women applied a sharpened saw blade to skim a layer off the rough cast surface, revealing a gleaming pewter finish. In the middle of the factory floor were tables where more craftspeople hammered row after precise row of indentations that were the only form of decoration at the time.

The shiny products were then packed using simple recycled materials. Up by the front door, employees wrenched the nails from used milk crates, sawed the planks down to size, and re-made them into boxes to pack the pewter. The precious pewter was carefully packed in yellow straw inside these reconstituted boxes.

Peng Kai, never satisfied, was always looking for ways to improve the pewter-making process. Upstairs, amongst the family's living quarters, was a secret room where Peng Kai carried out experiments

with machines. Among other things, it housed his first engraving machine, which he had bought second-hand in 1951 from the Malayan Railway workshop and modified so it could accommodate large items such as trophies. The room was out of bounds to everyone except his wife and his children, whom he taught to operate the engraving machine. Peng Kai had worked so hard to create a new industry out of an ancient craft, and he was anxious to keep his modern methods hidden from competitors.

The innovations went beyond the technical. Peng Kai's company was one of the first to hire women, some as young as 15. Before that, young girls worked as either maids or seamstresses. But he was progressive only to a point: in 1960, male workers earned about 3.20 Straits dollars a day while women earned about 1.30. The argument was that the men's work – such as casting pewter sheets and forming the pewter on a spinning lathe – required brute strength while the women's work – filing, scraping and polishing – did not.

The pewter shop on Batu Road became a popular stop for tourists and visiting celeb-

rities. In the early 1960s, American actor William Holden dropped in with French actress Capucine. They were filming "The Seventh Dawn", a film about an American soldier who led troops in Malaya during the Second World War and stayed on as a plantation owner only to find himself caught up in

A Selangor Pewter item with engraving was a most popular souvenir among British and Australian armed forces personnel in the 50s and 60s.

Opposite: Peng Kai and staff in the workshop at Pudu Road, 1960.

Poh Shin working a spinning lathe in the factory, 1960.

Opposite: Actors William Holden and Capucine at the pewter shop on Batu Road.

Following page: Pewter coffeepot, creamer and teapots with hammered decoration and rattan handles from the 1930s.

the country's war against communists. Capucine played his local love interest.

The film was a flop at the box office, but Mr Holden's visit was a boon for Selangor Pewter. The actor ended up placing a large order of cigarette cases as gifts for friends.

It was the biggest order the factory had ever received and it threw the workers into a flap as they rushed to complete the cases before filming in Malaysia ended.

Peng Kai worked alongside his employees, sweating through his Pagoda-brand white cotton vest and Western style trousers. Behind his back, the workers called him "Old Cowboy". His manner, though, was gentlemanly. Those who are still around remember that he always paid wages promptly and never raised his voice in anger, neither of which was normal behaviour for a Chinese employer at the time. "It was very usual for a Chinese businessman to scold and to use foul language," Hoo Wee Meng, who was employee number 29, said. In people like Wee Meng, who joined in 1960 as a young man of 20, Peng Kai inspired the sort of devotion seldom seen today. Peng Kai "treated us like family members," he said. "I worshipped him." □

'OUT IN THE STICKS':

PENG KAI'S NEW FACTORY

■ In 1962, Peng Kai made a leap of faith. He moved the company from the 2,000-square-foot shophouse in Pudu to a new 4,000-square-foot facility in a northern Kuala Lumpur suburb called Setapak.

Setapak was as remote as Pudu had been in the early days, and was known mainly for its therapeutic hot springs and for the leafy National Zoo nearby. It had one unexpected burst of glamour: the house of P. Ramlee, the late singer, actor and filmmaker whom many still regard as the most talented performer Malaysia has ever produced. Selangor Pewter's neighbours were a biscuit factory and a nail factory.

In that nondescript neighbourhood, Peng Kai's new facility was a revelation. In the past, many employees had often worried if

Selangor Pewter could survive. The company was certainly a strange creature. For one thing, the business was run out of an ordinary shophouse, which the neighbours erroneously called the "Silver Cup Factory". For another, it catered to a niche market of expatriates. Though the employees knew the products inside out, polishing each item by hand to a satin sheen, neither they nor anyone they knew actually used tankards, ashtrays or toast racks.

The new factory, with its updated machines, spacious factory floor, and rows of glass-paned windows that let in light and air, helped put those fears to rest.

The timing of the new factory was opportune. The Malaysian government, having been burnt by the vagaries of the world

Foreman Lai Woh taking delivery of tin ingots while security guard Mann Singh looks on, 1960s.

commodities markets, was anxious to lessen its economic reliance on rubber and tin as raw commodities. The government was eager to promote local industry and extended a helping hand to Peng Kai. He got a loan of 150,000 ringgit from Malaysian Industrial Development Finance, a government agency. (The loan caused Peng Kai sleepless nights until he paid back the last cent.)

In addition to cash, the government loaned Peng Kai three consultants from the International Labour Organization, who were in town to help Malaysia set up a National Productivity Centre. The company was growing beyond a cottage industry and was ripe for experiments in workflow and mechanization.

The consultants helped design the layout of the plant. They recommended seating postures and fixed the height of tables and shelves so employees could work comfortably without constantly bending or stretching. One of the consultants designed a new polishing contraption that ran on the electric motor of a sewing machine, which was far quieter than the old polishing machines that had rumbled and rattled all day in the Pudu Road factory.

The first new factory in Setapak, on the outskirts of Kuala Lumpur, 1962.

■ In many ways, the business retained its family-oriented air. Those who worked a late shift were treated to steaming bowls of sweet red bean soup from the family kitchen. On Lunar New Year, Peng Kai and Soh Eng distributed auspicious red money packets and mandarin oranges, a symbol of gold. The couple attended every employee wedding,

Opposite: The front of the new factory and company vehicles proudly advertising the product.

every "full moon" party – thrown by proud parents to mark their babies' first month – and every funeral.

The two often behaved like surrogate parents when it came to employee finances or safety. In fact, the staff called them "Auntie" and "Uncle", the usual form of deference for elders in many parts of Asia. The company ran a hostel in Setapak that housed 14 workers, so they wouldn't have to travel long distances to work. Once, when four high-spirited young female engravers went out dancing and broke their evening curfew, a worried Peng Kai dispatched his eldest son on a motorbike to retrieve them.

Soh Eng arranged for employees to open bank accounts so they could save money. Peng Kai encouraged them to use the money to invest in houses, often checking out new

housing projects himself and booking the homes for his workers. "Auntie always said: 'Must saving,'" remembers Mistiran Haji Redwan, who joined the company in 1963 at 19 years old.

One by one, Peng Kai's four children were being conscripted full-time into the business. Some were more willing than others, but in those days, family duty was more important than personal ambition. If he was mild-mannered with his employees, Peng Kai was strict with his own children.

The first-born, Poh Shin, had been an early rebel. Instructed to help out at the factory after school from age seven, he often sneaked out for a game of marbles with his friends. When he slunk back home, his furious father pulled him by the ear and caned him on the palm before the entire factory. The first day of transgression would earn him one stroke, the second consecutive day, two strokes, and so on. "We got up to ten strokes, then I learned my lesson," remembers Poh Shin. He'd stay home a few afternoons, and then the cycle would "start all over again".

When Poh Shin completed fifth form at 18, he wanted to be a cigarette salesman

One of the longest serving employees, Mistiran Haji Redwan, joined the company in 1963 at the age of 19.

for Rothmans. The job was irresistibly glamorous: it came with an entertainment allowance and, even more thrillingly, the use of a Ford Cortina station wagon. For someone who rode a Lambretta scooter, bought second-hand from his father, the idea of serious wheels was "a big thing".

His father wouldn't hear of it. Peng Kai told Poh Shin he needed him by his side. So Poh Shin worked on the factory floor, forming pewter items with the spinning lathe. After a few years, Peng Kai asked Poh Shin to run the Setapak factory. From 1964 to 1966, Poh Shin stationed himself in an elevated cockpit from where he could keep an eye on every employee.

Poh Shin had inherited his mother's gregariousness. He joined the Junior Chamber of Commerce, known as the Jaycees. Members, who were young professional men, took on community service projects ranging from repairing mosques to organizing the Miss Malaysia beauty pageant. At first, Peng Kai was unhappy with his son's extra-curricular jaunts, which he suspected were excuses to skip work. However, he soon changed his mind when Poh Shin's Jaycee

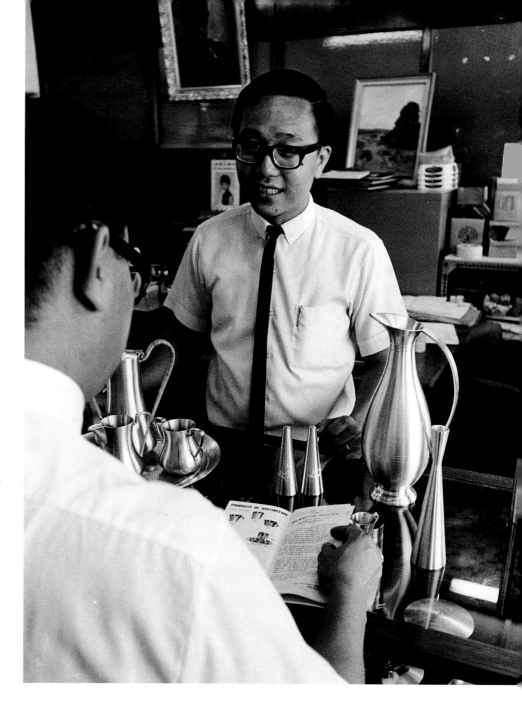

and other contacts came in handy for the company's expansion.

After two years of running the Setapak factory, Poh Shin began making regular visits to the company's retail partners, dropping in on shops in Singapore and Melaka. He chatted with the retailers and tried to persuade them to give Selangor Pewter bigger, more prominent displays. Often, Poh Shin roared in on his motorbike armed with swathes of blue satin, which he draped over boxes to create multi-tiered props on which to set off the gleaming pewter.

The company's biggest distributor at the time was a camera and watch shop called Lee Wah in Melaka that catered to Australian forces based in the nearby Terendak camp. When Poh Shin first visited the husband-and-wife team that ran the shop, Lee Wah had one shelf of pewter; pretty soon, that had expanded to half the shop. It was "purely relationship marketing," says Poh Shin.

■ Mun Ha, the elder daughter, was also enlisted after completing fifth form. At the time, the usual options for bright young women were teaching and nursing. The head of Mun Ha's school recommended that she go to Kirkby College in the UK, which trained many Malaysian teachers. Peng Kai said he couldn't spare her, and she too joined the company in 1958. Mun Ha remembers that both she and Poh Shin were paid 100 ringgit a month, of which 40 ringgit went back to their parents for food and lodging.

Mun Ha joined her mother in the Batu Road shop, taking over the book-keeping. It was a time of growth. "Every year, you saw the business improve," she remembers. To publicize the company's products, she joined the Advertisers' Association. In the 1960s, she was on the organizing committee of the association's annual ball, a highlight of the Kuala Lumpur social calendar. At the end of the evening, hundreds of attendees from large multinationals and local companies each took home a small bag of giveaways, which always included a Selangor Pewter key chain or small cup. "We put the product in front of them," she remembers. "Otherwise, how would anyone know there was a pewter company out there in the sticks?"

Opposite: Processess in the 1970s. Clockwise from top left: Foreman Lai Woh casting pewter sheets between iron slabs; "rolling" the cast pewter sheets; Supervisor Ah Joe Ee forming pewter objects with a spinning lathe; Lai Woh soldering the spout on a coffeepot.

Engraving is an essential part of the business, especially for commemoratives and awards.

These engraved napkin rings were very popular with tourists in the 60s and 70s.

In 1968, Selangor Pewter was doing well enough to graduate to its first full shop. The new shop was located at 231 Batu Road, down the street from the first half-shop and was run by Mun Ha. It was a milestone. The building was that of a typical Chinese shophouse but inside, the family began experimenting with the modern display arrangements that best showed off their pewter. For the first time, they did not have to settle for cramped displays. They did not have to plead with other retailers to fill a pewter bowl with fruit, or a vase with fresh flowers.

Over the years, Mun Ha would continue to be the most hands-on of the siblings when it came to the retail side of the business. In 1995, she opened the company's first wholly owned retail shop in Australia, in Melbourne's Block Arcade, displaying the same verve of the early years. "I opened on Sundays," she remembers. "We were paying rent anyway." That successful experiment led to the opening of several more shops in Melbourne and Brisbane.

But back around 1960, as the business prospered, the two younger siblings enjoyed progressively more leeway.

■ As a baby, Mun Kuen was often left bawling in a wooden milk crate in the old Pudu factory, with her parents sometimes too busy to change her nappies. She grew up to become the first in the family to complete sixth form (equivalent to high school in the US), at the Victoria Institution, a white-washed colonial landmark named after the English monarch. Peng Kai felt magnanimous enough to "lend" Mun Kuen to his great friend, Sun Sai Lum, who had retired as a police officer and was then running a detective agency. For several months, Mun Kuen answered phone calls and typed letters, assisting Sai Lum as he investigated insurance claims for car crashes. Then she joined her sister at the Batu Road shop.

In the 1960s and 1970s, Mun Kuen and her sister Mun Ha sold pewter to American soldiers on R&R from the Vietnam War. The soldiers bought beer mugs, cigarette boxes, cocktail shakers, fruit bowls, toast racks and casserole stands, to be packed and shipped to family and friends in the United States. The tourist trade grew as Malaysia aggressively promoted itself as a tropical paradise with white beaches, friendly people and a

Opposite: The shop at No. 231 Batu Road, Kuala Lumpur.

Selangor Pewter products were used as trophies and awards. Angela Filmer, Miss Malaysia 1964 and Miss Asia 1965.

Sixteen pewter water lilies for the National Monument in Kuala Lumpur, 1969.

Opposite: Wall mural commissioned by Bank Negara, Kuala Lumpur, and designed by Syed Ahmad Jamal. Poh Kon is seen discussing the project with the first Malaysian bank governor, Tun Ismail Ali. Kuala Lumpur, 1971.

The youngest sibling, Poh Kon, was in some ways the luckiest in the family. By then, the business had prospered enough for Peng Kai to have a little spare cash to send Poh Kon to university. Poh Kon studied mechanical engineering at the University of Adelaide in Australia. In the 1960s, Adelaide may as well have been at the other end of the world. The journey involved a flight to Perth, an overnight stay, followed by a ride on a propeller plane from Perth to Adelaide. Soh Eng cried when her youngest child left. When Poh Kon graduated in 1968, his parents flew to his side. The old man wore a dark Western-style suit and tie for the occasion while his wife wore a silk brocade jacket over a traditional Nonya *baju kebaya*, a lacy gauzy blouse and tight batik sarong, her hair up. After the ceremony, the normally taciturn Peng Kai told his youngest son: "My burden has been lifted."

There was now an engineer in the family. When Poh Kon returned to Malaysia in 1968, he began running the factory, freeing Poh Shin to start another Selangor Pewter factory in Singapore. Poh Kon introduced

mix of Malay, Chinese and Indian cultures. By the mid-1980s, the company had a small army of sales assistants to handle tourists in a growing network of shops. Mun Kuen switched to selling specially designed items to corporations, an increasingly important part of the business, and served VIP customers such as the Sultan of Selangor, who was to become a great supporter of the company.

Poh Kon with his parents when he graduated from the University of Adelaide in 1968.

new production processes, alloying metals for the first time and introducing hydraulic presses and other newfangled machinery.

■ In a way, Peng Kai and Soh Eng's children were emblematic of Malaysia's independence generation. They came of age at a time when the newly self-governing country was filled with hope and optimism. They were grounded by the family, but were also outward looking and ambitious. The generations before had been concerned chiefly with survival; this one was ready to soar. In the 1970s, with their children firmly installed, Peng Kai and Soh Eng gradually withdrew from company duties.

Peng Kai officially retired in 1980 and was feted with a grand dinner on December 14, 1980, the eve of his 65th birthday. The dinner, attended by 900 guests, was held at the Nirwana Ballroom of the Hilton, the best hotel in the city. The menu included braised egg noodles to signify longevity and an organist played "My Way". Peng Kai was presented with a pewter bust in his likeness. He blew out sixty-five red candles on a big cake, surrounded on stage by Soh Eng, their four children and respective spouses, and eleven grandchildren. The family had come a long way from their little shophouse on the fringe of the jungle.

But like so many people for whom work is everything, Peng Kai couldn't completely let go. He kept an office at the company's

headquarters and continued to lunch regularly in the executive dining room. In the end, it was ill health that stopped him from driving each day to the company he spent his life building. In November 1990, Peng Kai succumbed to motor neurone disease, an affliction that rapidly destroys the nerves controlling movement while leaving the mind and senses mostly unaffected.

Soh Eng took to retirement more readily, filling her days with her family and friends. Her pewter-coloured Honda Civic was always filled with live chickens, vegetables and grandchildren as she shopped and babysat for her busy children, all of whom had inherited their parents' work ethic. In 1990, she suffered a stroke and became bedridden. But even paralysed and unable to speak, she remained the emotional centre of the family, with her children and grandchildren gathering regularly by her bedside. She died in September 1995. □

Left and below: Peng Kai, at 65, surrounded by family unveils a pewter bust of himself at his retirement dinner in 1980.

Soh Eng, 1965

Innovations in pewtersmithing

Like his father and brother before him, Poh Kon was always looking for a better way to make pewter.

On his return to Kuala Lumpur, the young engineering graduate experimented with different metal alloys. Tin is a soft metal and in the past, lead was added to harden it. But lead is poisonous and, if swallowed, can be absorbed into the bloodstream. In some people, prolonged exposure can cause anaemia and high blood pressure, among other ailments. (Others show no symptoms.) Around the world, pewterers were starting to remove lead from their products, relying instead on small amounts of copper and antimony to counter the softness of tin.

Peng Kai had in the past been forced to rely on a commercial pre-mix composed of Straits-refined tin with antimony, copper and traces of lead. In 1968, Poh Kon changed the alloys, completely eliminating lead. Today, the company's pewter is composed of 97 per cent tin, 0.5 per cent antimony and 2.5 per cent copper.

The 1970s brought a significant advance in Malaysian pewter-making. Up until then, the company cast pewter sheets in the traditional Chinese way, between tiles. In 1972, the company signed a contract with Soltauer Zinngiesserei to manufacture the German company's pewter in Malaysia. The joint venture only lasted a few years, but it offered access to Soltauer Zinn's technology for casting pewter using steel moulds.

In a secret room on the second floor of a separate building, the company carried out experiments. The pewter alloy was heated to 350 degrees Celsius and the molten liquid poured into a mould. The mould was draped with a wet cloth or sprayed with water to help the pewter cool and solidify. The mould was then opened and the pewter object extracted. The new process was not just faster, it also

The raw material, Straits-refined tin.

Opposite: Former chief supervisor of the casting department Haji Wali Abdul Khalid casting tankards.

allowed for intricate profiles and textures to be cast from the mould.

Haji Wali Abdul Khalid was the first employee to be taught the new German technology. The son of Pakistani immigrants, who joined the company at age 18, he remembers those first heady days: "I couldn't believe it," he told the author. "It was a miracle."

Above: Medallions made for the
1998 Commonwealth Games.

Left: Validevi pours molten pewter
into a mould to form handles.

A German technician at the time said "you people are very lucky," remembers Chong Hong Chong, who was then factory supervisor. "This technology has never left Europe for two to three hundred years."

Casting pewter in steel moulds didn't just cut down on production time; it also made for stronger pewter objects. The old way of making pewter required that the pewter sheets be squeezed through rollers to reduce them to the thickness required. Unlike other metals, which harden when compressed, compressing pewter sheets breaks down the original crystal structure of the metal, weakening it slightly.

As such, pewter made from rolled sheets is usually less strong than pewter cast from moulds. One way of testing which method was used is to strike the pewter object with a pencil; pewter cast in a mould has a bell-like ring.

Poh Kon continued the process of mechanization that his father started. Often, he employed technology that had never been used for pewter, borrowing from other industries. During a visit to the Japan Expo in Osaka in 1970, Poh Kon was "astounded" by the number of people who bought copper and aluminium medallions, which were anodized with silver, gold and bronze. On his return, he made a trip to Singapore, to visit the Light Industrial Services workshop of Singapore's Economic Development Board. Singapore was promoting light industries to generate employment and at the workshop were machines for engraving three-dimensional moulds, mainly for the plastic and shoe industries.

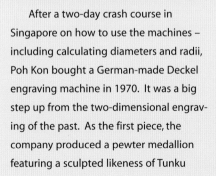

Left to right: Koh Shoon soldering a vase;
Chin Yoke Lan hammering decorative indentations
on a tankard; Esah Jantan polishing pewter.

After a two-day crash course in Singapore on how to use the machines – including calculating diameters and radii, Poh Kon bought a German-made Deckel engraving machine in 1970. It was a big step up from the two-dimensional engraving of the past. As the first piece, the company produced a pewter medallion featuring a sculpted likeness of Tunku Abdul Rahman, the first prime minister of Malaysia. Over the years, the company has produced medals for the Commonwealth Games, the Southeast Asian Games and numerous tournaments and awards.

In the 1970s, Poh Kon bought lathe machines with hydraulic copiers that could turn out a shape according to a template. After an object was cast in a mould, these machines were used to skim off a thick layer to reveal a shiny surface. Computerized lathes were added in the 1980s, which allowed for greater uniformity and precision in the products. The lids of tea caddies, for example, require a snug fit since an airtight environment preserves the tea leaves.

These and other innovations allowed Selangor Pewter to overcome the limitations of the old pewtersmiths and to branch into new products and new markets. Yet despite the new machines, much still rides on human skill and expertise. Today, the pewter is still cast by hand and parts are soldered by hand by experienced craftspeople. Finally, every piece is polished by hand.

BUILDING A BRAND:
'MALAYA'S SUPERFINE PRODUCT'

Coffee set from the
Royal Collection, one
of Anders Quistgaard's
first designs for
Selangor Pewter, 1981.

■ An interviewer once asked Peng Kai who
was responsible for new designs. He replied
that he was, as were his sons and daughters.
When he was asked if there was any sort of
system to his early catalogue numbers, he
answered: "Nothing!" To the question "How
did you decide to stop producing something?"
he said: "We don't stop! We add on, we add
on," paused, and emphasized, "we add on."

That pretty much summed up the state
of affairs from the 1940s through to the early
1970s. The company was innovative and
always quick to seize on new notions and
sales opportunities. But one result of that
early gung ho attitude was that there was
often little time for planning.

Peng Kai certainly had many marketing
ideas ahead of his time.

The end of the Second World War, for
example, saw Peng Kai producing his first
commemorative souvenirs. One of the first
things he did after the British made a tri-
umphant return to Malaya was to cast
pewter V-shaped victory badges, painted the
white, red and blue of the Union Jack, for
attaching to the front of motorcars. In 1946
and 1947, Peng Kai modified his pewter
tankards to include the year next to the
Selangor Pewter stamp. The simple addition
of a date transformed regular tankards into
sentimental keepsakes for members of the
British military.

In the 1950s, the tone of his marketing efforts changed in tune with the new era of peace and prosperity. Peng Kai flirted with direct mail, sending brochures as far away as America and Germany with the promise that "Malaya's Superfine Product" would "beautify the nicest home" and "make hearts thrillingly happy". Eldest son Poh Shin further honed these marketing programmes, putting together some of the first catalogues. He shot black-and-white photographs of the pewter designs with a Yashica camera, handwrote catalogue numbers, got the catalogues printed and sent them out to "agents", shops owned by others that stocked Selangor Pewter and earned a commission from each sale.

By the late 1960s, the product with the early tagline "Malaysia's Gift to the World" was growing beyond its core expatriate and tourist market. Poh Shin moved to Singapore in 1968 to set up a second pewter factory, bringing his young family with him a year later. In the 1970s, Australia became a big export market for the company, particularly for pewter beer mugs. Back in Malaysia, besides a growing number of "dealers", the company's client list now included a

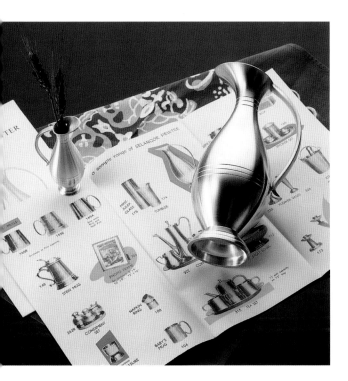

Opposite: Mun Ha, late 1950s.

Over the years, Selangor Pewter's marketing brochures and packaging gradually became more sophisticated.

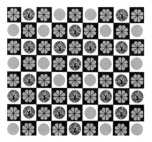

ately inducted into the pewter business. On their first day under Peng Kai's roof, the two little girls were each presented with a stack of printed receipt books. The year was almost over and Peng Kai, ever frugal, instructed them to change the "7" in 1957 to an "8" so the books could be used into the new year. "People talk about child labour," Boon Lay said years later, laughing: "but it was about being involved."

Peng Kai quickly recognized Boon Lay's talent for drawing and painting. He arranged for the child to attend art classes. When Boon Lay was 17, the Yong family sent her to Bristol Art College in the UK. The Yongs were reluctant to wait too long for their protégé to return. As it turned out, the college principal was a former British air force pilot who was shot down over Malaya and rescued by locals during the war. He obliged by allowing Boon Lay a shortened art and design course of 20 months, with an emphasis on metalwork.

In 1972, Boon Lay returned to Kuala Lumpur. Working from a rooftop studio above the factory, she designed tulip-shaped goblets, which became a best seller and

substantial corporate component, with entities ranging from multinationals to government agencies and sports associations.

■ With business booming, it was clear that the company's design and marketing efforts had to be formalized in some way. The family had already identified an ideal candidate: Soh Eng's niece, Guay Boon Lay.

Boon Lay and Boon Kiow, daughters of Soh Eng's brother, had moved in with the family in Pudu in 1957 when they were old enough to attend school. They were immedi-

Right: Anders Quistgaard, 1985.

Upon her return from studying in the UK, Soh Eng's niece, Boon Lay, headed Selangor Pewter's design department for a number of years. 1973.

remain in production today. She designed corporate gifts for companies. And she created professional catalogues and brochures. In 1976, the company hired a young Dane named Anders Quistgaard, who had previously designed tableware for Danish ceramics company Bing & Grøndahl. Anders was the son of Jens Quistgaard, who in 1954 won the Lunning Prize, which honours Scandinavian design.

Anders' assignment was to come up with modern packaging for the pewter, based on modular dimensions that fit the export pallet. Selangor Pewter's Australian agent had complained about the reconfigured milk carton packaging, with its yellow straw that spilled out and made a mess on unpacking. Anders designed cardboard boxes with a blue and white "lapis lazuli" print, each with a diamond-shaped logo containing the legend "1885", the year of the patriarch Yong Koon's arrival in Malaya. He did away with the straw and had the pewter pieces wrapped instead in tissue and a thin layer of foam before they were placed in the signature blue boxes.

In 1978, Anders joined Selangor Pewter full-time. Together with Boon Lay, who had become his wife, they created the company's first real design department.

It was a period of rapid growth and the factory that had seemed so large in the early 1960s was bursting at the seams. In 1977, the company moved to a 12-acre site five minutes away, with its own football field. The factory floor covered 60,000 square feet and there were 300 employees.

Anders, who was as temperamental as he was talented, was chief designer. He set up a model shop, to make prototypes of new products. The model shop is headed today by Boon Lay's brother, Guay Chin Huat. Anders introduced a House Design Committee to evaluate new designs for production. Boon Lay produced catalogues and brochures.

Long-time employees remember Anders' creative energy, versatility and dedication. "I once asked Anders what makes a good designer," says Tan Jooi Chong, who joined the design department in 1980. "He simply said: 'Understanding the craft.'"

But he wasn't all seriousness. Janet Siew, who joined the company in 1976, remembers a man who ended every meeting with a "goody goody good" and a wide grin.

Up till the 1970s, the pewter came only in a brushed finish known as "satin". Anders designed a teapot in the Queen Anne style and gave it a high polish akin to silver, then added a sugar bowl, creamer and tray to make up a Royal Collection. He experimented with new materials. He had studied traditional wooden architecture in Japan and combined wood and pewter to create a range of men's accessories, which he called The Admiral Line. To ensure the quality and

supply of wood for the range, he started a wood workshop.

In 1985, the company's centenary, he conceived of a project that initially drew incredulous looks within the company: The Giant Tankard. Ignoring the protests, Anders went ahead and calculated the logistics around the project. The tankard was cast in four separate pieces at an iron foundry and the parts soldered together. It was 1.987 metres tall and weighed 1,557 kilograms. It had a capacity of 2,796 litres or a whopping 4,920 pints of beer. The tankard was listed in the Guinness Book of World Records for several years, generated a lot of newsprint, and became a big draw for tourists to the factory.

The lapis lazuli packaging created by Anders.

■ Selangor Pewter was now a top tourist stop in Malaysia. Its exports were growing. But the company was looking for a stronger global presence.

In 1986, the company commissioned Erik Magnussen to design a line aimed at Western markets. Erik was a design icon known for his cylindrical tableware in plastic and stainless steel for the Danish company Stelton and his furniture for Fritz Hansen. Erik had heard of the Malaysian company but had never worked with pewter.

He was excited by the challenge posed by the metal. Erik's design philosophy is to make things easier to use. Since pewter is a relatively soft metal, Erik added a little edge at the bottom or top of his designs as a sort of bumper to protect the shiny cylindrical walls of his creations. "The softness of the material influenced the shape," says Erik. "The challenge was to make a modern design and still respect the material."

With their niche appeal, Erik's pewter creations – tableware and desk accessories – didn't sell in huge numbers, but they were important in that they attracted the attention of serious design aficionados. Items

from the collection won design awards at the Frankfurt International Gift Fair in 1989 and in 1991. The Museum of Modern Art in New York sold the items in its museum shop for several years, as did the Copenhagen design store Illums Bolighus.

Anders and Boon Lay stayed until 1987, when they moved to Denmark, where Anders became ill with leukaemia. He died in 2000. Under the structure that they left behind, the company's in-house Malaysian designers began rolling out new ranges every year. □

Opposite: Anders and Boon Lay created an in-house design studio, pictured here in 1979.

The Giant Tankard, a pet project of Anders' that caused some controversy within the company when the idea was first proposed, found a place in the Guinness Book of World Records as the world's largest pewter tankard.

Design Icons

Royal Selangor has won many awards around the world, gaining recognition over the years for its non-traditional use of pewter, for combining pewter with other materials, and for sheer beauty of design.

Anders Quistgaard, head of the company's design department for a decade up to 1987, pushed the boundaries of pewter design and fostered an abiding culture of innovation that has won the company a string of product awards up until today.

Admiral Line

The Admiral line was based on the traditional captain's chest, where the captain kept maps, inks and feather quills. Launched in 1982, it was the first collection aimed at men, and included cigarette boxes, lighters, ashtrays and desk accessories. Anders had studied traditional wooden architecture in Japan and was eager to apply his knowledge to combining wood and pewter. He designed the products with pewter shims, or corners, that were both decorative and served to hold the wooden parts together. The Admiral line won a New and Improved Product Development Award from the Federation of Malaysian Manufacturers in 1983.

The Sovereign Collection

Inspired by classic silver designs, The Royal Collection was introduced in 1981 and later renamed the Sovereign Collection. Anders based the tea and coffee pots on the Queen Anne design, added a sugar bowl and creamer, and polished the pewter to a mirror-like finish that was vastly different from pewter's usual satin sheen. The Sovereign Collection won a New and Improved Product Development Award in 1981 from the Federation of Malaysian Manufacturers and a Gold Medal in the Excellence in Quality and Design category at the Leipzig International Fair in Germany in 1984.

Erik Magnussen

Erik Magnussen is known for his cylindrical steel and plastic tableware for Stelton and furniture for Fritz Hansen. His collection for Royal Selangor was the first time he had worked with pewter and bears the hallmarks of the Danish designer's style: clean cylindrical shapes that were easy to use. Pewter is a relatively soft metal and Erik devised a small edge at the bottom or top of his designs as a bumper to protect the highly polished walls. Tableware from the range won a Design Plus Award at the Frankfurt International Gift Fair in 1989 and an EM hipflask won a Design Plus Award in 1991.

Nick Munro

UK designer Nick Munro, who launched his career by turning bed springs into egg cups, fused Eastern and Western designs for his groundbreaking work with Royal Selangor.

What looks like a smooth beach pebble reveals itself as a pencil sharpener. Photo frames take on the gentle swaying lines of marsh grasses. And a small pewter turtle is actually a tooth box.

Five Elements

In his Five Elements range, Hong Kong designer Freeman Lau drew on traditional Chinese philosophy to emerge with modern design.

In China, the five elements of wood, fire, earth, metal and water symbolize balance, leading to harmony, growth and prosperity.

Freeman created abstract symbols for the elements to grace incense burners, photo frames and other tabletop pieces.

Wine Funnel

Part of Royal Selangor's contemporary Wine Celebration range, this funnel serves to aerate the wine as it flows in a graceful arc into the crystal decanter. Christopher Ponniah, Royal Selangor's former head of product development, oversaw the development of the wine funnel from a germ of an idea to triple award winner. In 2003, the wine funnel garnered a *red dot* award for product design from the North Rhine-Westphalia Design Centre in Essen, Germany, a bronze Industrial Design Excellence Award in the consumer products category from the Industrial Designers Society of America, and a G-Mark Good Design Award from the Japan Industrial Design Promotion Organization.

Four Gentlemen

In Chinese art and poetry, the plum blossom, orchid, chrysanthemum and bamboo are said to embody the virtues of a Confucian scholar or gentleman. Inspired by these symbols, veteran Royal Selangor designer Tan Jooi Chong created the "Four Gentlemen" collection of tableware.

Plus

Sleek and tactile, the Plus range of personal accessories introduced Royal Selangor to a new, younger audience. Designed by Christopher Yong, a great-grandson of the company's founder, the pieces can be worn around the neck, turned into charms or key chains, or used to cinch a belt or bag.

GOING GLOBAL:

SARONG-CLAD PROMOTERS AND A ROYAL ADMIRER

■ People often ask how Royal Selangor survived two world wars, numerous recessions, and seismic shifts in style and fashion. The short answer is entrepreneurial spirit and a knack for innovation.

Looking back on its almost 120-year history, there are several junctures where the enterprise stood on shaky ground. Yet it always recovered. Each time, it reinvented itself for a different market…while maintaining its soul as a maker of high-quality pewter.

In the 1930s, when demand for Chinese ceremonial pieces was shrinking, the company shifted its focus to Western-style products for European expatriates. Instead of joss stick holders and candlesticks, the pewtersmiths began making tankards and cigarette cases. In the 1950s and 1960s, as Malaysia hunkered down to the job of setting up its own government and the number of expatriates dwindled, the pewter company turned its attention to the tourists who were just discovering Malaysia's beaches, jungles and varied cultures. To extend its sales network beyond Kuala Lumpur, the company recruited "agents" around Malaysia and Singapore that stocked its pewter and took a small commission on each sale.

The enterprise soon learnt the dangers of relying on tourists. In 1969, bloody race riots involving Malays and Chinese in Kuala Lumpur led to a virtual halt in tourist arrivals. For a few harrowing months that year, the factory worked a three- or four-day week, unsure if it could pull through. For the first time, the company laid off workers, a painful experience for an enterprise that regarded its employees as family.

Peng Kai and Poh Kon at the Tokyo International Trade Fair, 1970s.

To cool ethnic tensions, the Malaysian government drew up a sweeping affirmative action policy offering preferential treatment to native Malays in areas such as education, jobs and stock market share allocations. In this way, the government hoped to redress the wealth imbalance between the poorer Malay majority and the richer Chinese minority. The tourists returned, but the experience "drove home the importance of having a larger and more diversified market base," says Yong Poh Kon.

That realization led to a quest for wider markets that began in the 1970s and continues today. Designing for a global market was one part of the equation; introducing new production processes was another. The third and final part was building a physical presence in various countries.

Not all the company's foreign forays were successful – it has opened and closed offices in Switzerland and Denmark – but the lessons learnt along the way have been instructive. In 1970, less than two per cent of the company's production was exported; in 2000, Royal Selangor exported more than 60 per cent of its output.

Selangor Pewter's first foreign market was, predictably, Singapore. In 1968, attracted by Singaporean investment incentives, Yong Poh Shin moved to the island state to set up another Selangor Pewter factory.

Singapore had split from Malaysia in 1965 after an unhappy two years of merger. At the time, the island at the southern tip of the Malaysian peninsula was nothing like the regional financial and technology hub it is today. The Urban Redevelopment Authority had yet to tear down the old, low-rise shophouses and squatter colonies that dotted the island and replace them with super-efficient blocks of apartments and glass skyscrapers. In those days, Singapore's aspirations were as modest as those of any young third-world country were and its government was trying hard to attract labour-intensive industries through a combination of investment incentives and duties on imports.

With its reliance on handwork, Selangor Pewter qualified for these incentives. So Poh Shin set up a small pewter factory in Paya Lebar, so close to Singapore's former international airport that he could hear aeroplanes land and take off. The factory was

surrounded by attap huts and a pig farm. Eight employees from Kuala Lumpur accompanied him to Singapore. They slept on foldaway canvas beds at the factory, the women upstairs and the men downstairs. Employee Saleh Haji Hassan, a Malaysian who followed Poh Shin to Singapore initially for "six months, then eight months, then forever", remembers that neighbouring areas were filled with gangsters: "If they didn't like you, they beat you up."

Above left: 1966 advertisement of Selangor Pewter products.

Above: A retail catalogue, tourist edition, 1975.

Opposite: Early promotions. The Malaysian High Commission organized a display at the YWCA Christmas Fair in London, November 1966. Selangor Pewter was selected among other handicrafts.

This 1971 catalogue included "Products of Distinction for Gifts and Souvenirs", such as beer mugs with teakwood, whisky measures, egg cups, toast racks, ice pails, tongs and finger bowls.

Right: Brochures from the 1970s and 1980s.

This first group of employees trained Singaporean workers and the factory rapidly expanded. By the early 1970s, it ran into a problem: the factory was producing too many pieces for the Singapore market to absorb. At the time, distribution was handled by Orient Crafts, which was owned by the Melwani family. (The Melwanis are best known today for their fashion business in Singapore; they control franchises for Levi's, Escada and Liz Claiborne, amongst others.)

Orient Crafts distributed the pewter to the household names of that era: Mulchand's, Mohan's, China Crafts and Bobby-O. Poh Shin figured the fastest way to grow was to take back control of distribution. B.H. Melwani, who was then managing director of Orient Crafts, remembers the handover. Pewter "was only one of our businesses" says Mr Melwani. "But to them, it was their only business. We could understand."

New to town, Poh Shin enlisted the help of a distant relative named Ah Thian, who "knew Singapore and knew the roads". Driving Poh Shin's Mazda, Ah Thian delivered pewter to about 20 agents around the island. By the mid-70s, business was so good that there were 120 workers in the Singapore factory, compared to 200 at headquarters in Malaysia.

In 1993, Poh Shin moved the factory to the industrial district of Jurong, in southwestern Singapore. Since the late 1980s however, as tiny Singapore transformed itself against the odds into an Asian economic dynamo, its success has led to the

demise of the labour-intensive industries it once courted. The Singapore dollar has strengthened against the Malaysian ringgit and it is no longer cost-effective to manufacture pewter there.

Today, while the Singapore market remains an important one, the factory has ceased production and all pewter is imported from Malaysia.

Singapore, the company's first foray abroad, was at least familiar territory. Its proximity to Malaysia, shared history and similar culture meant that the same design and marketing criteria could often be applied to both markets. In trying to take on other countries though, the company waded into unknown waters.

■ While there were indigenous pewter-makers in the UK, France, Germany, the US and China, they have tended to remain very small and very local. For the most part, these traditional pewterers produce the same classic designs year after year, using the same trusted tools. As a result, although their pewter is valued by a small group of high-end jewellers and collectors, the market is shrinking – many

have closed – and young people in these countries prefer modern materials such as ceramic, glass or stainless steel.

For the Yong siblings, there was no globalization template to follow. With the relatively shorter history of pewter in Malaysia, perhaps it was easier to look to the future instead of the past. They tried different approaches – from appointing or setting up distribution companies to acquiring companies with related businesses to opening their own retail shops.

Almost from the start, Australia was an important market because of its proximity. From 1970, the company took part in sales conferences in Australia, where local sales representatives were introduced to new products. Malaysian government incentives for promoting exports led to a marketing budget being put aside for the first pewter advertisements on Australian television. The company sold thousands of goblets and tankards in Australia through major department stores such as Myer and David Jones, as well as jewellers and gift shops. In 1977, Selangor Pewter set up an Australian sales subsidiary in Melbourne.

Retail catalogue, 1990s.

Some of the publications and magazines which have helped to promote the brand name internationally, throughout the 1970s and 1980s.

Advertisement for a promotion at the Hudson's Bay Company, 1975.

Opposite: Advertisements and newspaper clippings record Selangor Pewter's global presence. Global ambassadors Lelie Lim and Tina Lee Saw-Ean in Copenhagen, Denmark, 1982. Helena Cheah and Jenny Hor Noi in Sydney and Ballarat, Australia, 1977.

Australia was the first "Western" market and offered a test bed for tailoring a product range aimed at non-Asian customers.

Other Western markets followed. One early attempt exemplified both the pioneering spirit of the time and the forces the small Malaysian company was up against.

In the mid-1970s, Poh Kon flew to Toronto to test the Canadian market. For the occasion, Boon Lay modified a large brown leather trunk for carrying pewter samples. The case was lined with foam and the felt-wrapped pewter pieces carefully placed inside. The trunk was heavy, so Poh Kon attached two small metal wheels to one corner.

Poh Kon's first meeting was with a buyer for Henry Birks & Sons, Canada's largest jewellery chain. Impressed by the quality of the pewter from the little-known Malaysian company, Birks immediately ordered 100 coffee sets. Poh Kon was elated.

The next meeting went less smoothly. Poh Kon made a presentation to the Hudson's Bay Company, a Canadian institution which had started as a fur-trading concern in 1670 and had evolved into one of the country's biggest retailers, selling all manner of items.

Sceptical, the company's merchandising manager quizzed Poh Kon on whether Selangor Pewter would still exist in five years. It was April 1975 and every day, television images showed US forces retreating from Vietnam. The domino theory was popular: that Vietnam's fall to communism would take down Cambodia, Thailand, Malaysia and Singapore in quick succession. Poh Kon assured the executive that Malaysia was safely capitalistic and would be for years to come, and the Hudson's Bay Company made its first order of Selangor Pewter for its department stores. (It remains a customer today.) As Poh Kon pulled his heavy trunk out of the lobby, his elation turned to horror. The metal wheels on his makeshift salesman's kit had gouged a visible trail on the shiny marble floor. Poh Kon fled.

It was this sort of early legwork, coupled with sheer persistence and a refusal to take no for an answer that enabled the company to break into new markets. In the mid-1970s, Poh Kon remembers, he and Poh Shin were on the road four to five months a year,

Malaysian girls show the beauty of pewter

Current interest in pewter is being stimulated this week by on-the-spot demonstrations of the skill and methods involved in finishing polishing and engraving the metal.

Two attractive young women from the Selangor Pewter Company of Kuala Lumpur are in Ballarat this week to conduct demonstrations at Thomas Jewellers.

The two women, Helena Cheah, a senior sales assistant from the firm's pewter demonstration centre, and Jenny Hor, a demonstrator who has been with the firm for 10 years, have spent the past month in Melbourne.

Similar visits have been paid to the capital cities in Australia for several years, but this is the first occasion in which a provincial centre has been included.

Their demonstrations, which attracted considerable interest in the store yesterday, will be continued today, and a competition being held in connection with the visit will be drawn shortly before they leave Ballarat on Thursday morning.

Many people yesterday paused to watch Jenny Hor at work with the soft metal, which is now 97 per cent tin, beating, polishing and engraving goblets, tankards, serviette rings and other small items.

ABOVE: Mr James Thomas discusses the beauty of pewter with Helena Cheah while her colleague demonstrator Jenny Hor, puts finishing touches to a goblet.

knocking on doors. The longest trip lasted six weeks and stretched across Canada from Toronto to Montreal to Edmonton – where the thermometer read minus 18 degrees Celsius; "my ears felt like they could snap off!" remembers Poh Kon – and on to Vancouver. In those years, Poh Kon hardly saw his wife and three small children.

To establish an industry presence, Selangor Pewter began participating in international gift and tableware fairs, important venues for establishing credibility as a manufacturer and for introducing new product lines to buyers.

These gatherings are invaluable for meeting representatives from the biggest department stores, jewellers and other retailers. In the 1970s, Selangor Pewter began showing its products at the Frankfurt International Gift Fair, the most important one for the industry. The company has since added Birmingham, Toronto, New York, Chicago, Los Angeles and Melbourne to its annual fair circuit.

■ Those were also the years when the company was building links with industry and international organizations. Poh Kon founded the Malaysia chapter of the Young Presidents Organisation, whose members are a "who's who" of global chief executives under 40. He also founded the Malaysia chapter of Mensa International, a society for people who score within the top two per cent of the population on a standardized intelligence test. Locally, the company was actively involved in the Federation of Malaysian Manufacturers, an influential

The company participated actively in trade exhibitions, locally and abroad. FMM - Federation of Malaysian Manufacturers - Award Winner, Kuala Lumpur, 1976.

industry group that often helps shape government economic policies and regulations.

Putting the products on retail shelves was a start, but it was not enough. The company needed to direct customers to those products. To do so, it embarked on a sort of "Singapore Girl" marketing approach. Only instead of smiling female flight attendants from Singapore Airlines in batik costume, Selangor Pewter sent forth smiling female pewtersmiths in batik costume.

From the mid-1970s, the company plucked these ambassadors from the factory floor and flew them around the world, stationing them in department stores for weeks at a time. Two "promoters", usually young women wearing batik *baju kebaya*, the long, shapely Malay dress, set up a booth in a high-traffic area within the store. They were as glamorous as they were skilled in engraving, polishing and answering questions on the products. Their props included a video, entitled "A Thing of Beauty", that showed the different stages of pewter making from casting to polishing. There was a portable machine that had a polishing head on one side and a wooden chuck on the other for hammering decorations. One promoter polished or hammered or engraved, while the other explained the process to passing shoppers.

The promoters attracted a lot of attention. "On Wednesday, we were interviewed in Cantonese and Mandarin by Radio Australia," June Hoh Chong Meng wrote from the Southern Cross Intercontinental Hotel in Melbourne, in a letter dated 27 October, 1975. The letter is peppered with the wide-eyed observations of a first time visitor: "Weather is very, very cold…people still put on warm clothings and goodness you should see them walk! If I am not mistaken, they walk fast is because of the coldness…[sic]."

Often, Yong Mun Ha herself embarked on these trips. A newspaper advertisement in the Australian newspaper *The Sun* in 1981, announces dates and times for pewter making demonstrations at a Myer departmental store in Burwood, a Sydney suburb. Next to a photo of a smiling Mun Ha is the caption: "The third generation of the pewter industry in Malaysia."

But a promoter's job wasn't all glamour. Wong Suet Mui, who was hired as a 15-year-old

Norrelah bte Md Noor and Sun Mun Ha featured in an advertisement in the Australian newspaper *The Sun* in 1981.

A view of the production floor
at headquarters in Setapak,
Kuala Lumpur, 1987.

at the Pudu factory in 1966, remembers the gruelling schedules. Starting in 1984, she made many trips to Japan, with the frequency peaking at two months each year between 1995 and 1998. On these trips, she set up her booth in Japanese department stores, offering to engrave an inscription without charge for every product bought. If sales were brisk, she engraved up to 50 pieces a day, sometimes taking the goblets and tankards back to her hotel room and working in the bathroom, where the light was brightest.

The effect of these promoters on branding has been as potent as the best television or magazine advertisements. As the number of such forays increased, the company was getting noticed, internationally, and at home. In the late 1970s, one of those who noticed was the Sultan of Selangor, His Royal Highness Sultan Salahuddin Abdul Aziz Shah. In 1979, the Sultan appointed the company royal pewterer and in 1992, Selangor Pewter officially changed its name to Royal Selangor. ☐

Royal Selangor stand at the National Exhibition Centre, Birmingham Spring Fair, 2002.

Left: Selangor Pewter headquarters 1987. In 1992, the name was changed to Royal Selangor.

Following page: The Sultan tries his hand at decorative hammering, 1979.

The Sultan and the pewter company

His Royal Highness Sultan Salahuddin Abdul Aziz Shah, the late Sultan of Selangor, was one of nine hereditary rulers in Malaysia. In the 1970s, the Sultan had been an occasional customer of Selangor Pewter, buying a pewter tea set for a visiting head of state or picking up a few gifts for a trip abroad. Once, he ordered pewter coasters engraved with a picture of his yacht to present to friends who boarded the vessel.

In the late 1970s, the Sultan was travelling in Perth, Australia, where he had a house. He stepped into a large department store with his entourage in tow and was respectfully asked by the sales assistants where he was from.

"Selangor," the Sultan answered.

"Ah, Selangor Pewter," the sales staff intoned. The Sultan was tickled that the Australians had heard of Selangor Pewter but not of the state of Selangor, nor of the Sultan of Selangor.

On his return, he decided that the pewter company should have royal status. In 1979, he conferred a royal warrant on Selangor Pewter. After that, he insisted that every pewter piece he bought be engraved with the words: "By royal appointment to his Royal Highness The Sultan of Selangor."

Yong Mun Kuen personally attended to the Sultan. Palace officials would telephone the day before and announce that the Sultan would arrive at 9.00 am the next morning at the company's headquarters in Setapak. He was always punctual, showing up in a casual safari suit. "He would look around and say 'I want two of this, I want six of that; mugs, trays, vases,'" remembers Mun Kuen. As soon as Mun Kuen tallied the purchases, he would invariably say "too much", knock about 30 per cent off the sum quoted, and write out a cheque for the amount. After all, he was the Sultan.

When the Sultan celebrated 25 years on the throne, he commissioned Selangor Pewter to make small pewter badges with his portrait sculptured in relief. He ordered 350,000 badges and gave them to every schoolchild in the state of Selangor. For VIPs, the Sultan ordered medals with his portrait on one side and his official crest on the other.

In 1992, in recognition of the royal warrant, the company officially changed its name to Royal Selangor.

The Sultan passed away in December 2001, after he was hospitalized for heart problems. His son, Sultan Sharafuddin Idris Shah, succeeded him.

By appointment to
HRH The Sultan of Selangor
Royal Pewterer
Royal Selangor International Sdn Bhd

ROYAL SELANGOR TODAY

Above: The Suria KLCC shopping centre, located at the foot of the Petronas Twin Towers, is home to one of Royal Selangor's retail stores.

Right: Romanza diamond rings from Selberan in white and yellow gold.

Opposite: Royal Selangor's 125th anniversary was marked by the opening of its flagship store in Pavilion Kuala Lumpur in 2010.

■ The Royal Selangor enterprise has come a long way from its beginnings in a little shophouse on Cross Street.

While in Yong Koon's day a single pewtersmith crafted a teapot or a wine ewer from beginning to end, today's gleaming products owe their shape and lustre to a team that includes designers, model makers, mould makers and engineers. Yet, true to its tradition of craftsmanship, every piece is polished and finished by hand by experienced pewterers, some of whom joined the company in the 1960s as teenagers.

New designs are introduced each year and sold around the world through retail stores and online.

Over the years, Royal Selangor has grown into the biggest pewtermaker in the world

and expanded into silver and gold. It has also formed partnerships and acquired some established companies along the way.

As early as 1972, the company formed a joint venture with a Swiss master jeweller, Werner Eberhard, and an Austrian gem setter, Walter Angelmahr, to start a jewellery business. Selberan, a name coined from the three words Selangor, Eberhard and Angelmahr, was one of the first Malaysian companies to manufacture jewellery to European design and standards, developing over the years into a brand name in its own right with shops in Kuala Lumpur.

In 1987, the company acquired Englefields, the 300-year-old London maker of Crown & Rose pewter. Englefields has

Pewter paperweights crafted by Royal Selangor for US outdoor lifestyle brand Timberland.

Right: The Asian Football Confederation trophy made by Comyns, in sterling silver, 2003.

now been renamed Royal Selangor UK. In 1993, Royal Selangor acquired the London silver company Comyns, along with some 35,000 historic silver designs dating back to the 17th century. Alongside the historical designs, Comyns designers and silversmiths now also produce contemporary silver pieces including jewellery.

■ Custom designs have also become an integral part of the business. The company designs and makes trophies, medals, souvenirs and gifts for corporations and individuals, drawing on its expertise in different precious metals.

Royal Selangor manufactured champagne buckets for LMVH Moët Hennessy, the French purveyor of luxury goods. The company's pewtersmiths made Formula 1 trophies for the Malaysia, Singapore and China Grand Prix while Comyns silver-smiths crafted a silver trophy for the Asian Football Confederation.

When Sultan Sharafuddin Idris Shah succeeded his father as Sultan of Selangor in 2003, he commissioned sets of gold-plated silver postage stamps as a way to

thank donors to his foundation for underprivileged youths. Selberan, Royal Selangor's jewellery company, played a backstage role, refitting and refurbishing the Sultan's crown for his coronation ceremony.

As its customers have grown, so too has the organization. From a cottage industry where employees addressed their bosses as "Auntie" and "Uncle", Royal Selangor has transformed itself into a modern, professionally run corporation.

The Sultan's Stamp Collection

From his personal collection, Sultan
Sharafuddin Idris Shah selected 16 postage
stamps depicting historical Selangor rulers
and landmarks spanning over a century.
Royal Selangor sculpted these images in
perfect detail and minted the stamps in
solid 999 silver ingots gilded in 24K gold.

The Sultan's Crown

The Sultan of Selangor's magnificent gold
crown has been in his family since 1826 and
has become as much a part of the coronation ceremony as the gold-threaded yellow
songket suit and *keris*, the wavy dagger
symbolizing the Malay warrior. For Sultan
Sharafuddin Idris Shah's coronation in 2003,
Selberan jewellers polished and refitted
the crown, maintaining the integrity of the
original intricate goldwork. They added
diamonds and rubies for greater sparkle.

These changes continue today. Among other things, the company has formalized different departments, hired non-family members to head them, implemented computerized tracking systems for manufacturing, warehousing and distribution, and introduced online sales.

■ Today, the family shares responsibilities with a team of non-family professionals. Overall, Poh Kon remains chief executive and day-to-day operations come under

executive directors Yong Yoon Li and Chen Tien Yue, both great-grandchildren of the founder. Before joining the family company, Yoon Li spent nine years in the automotive and motorsports industries in the UK and Malaysia, including as general manager of sports car maker TVR in Kuala Lumpur. Tien Yue is a former consultant with the management consultancy McKinsey & Co. The board includes two other, non-family, executives. CY Wong, who joined the company in 1984, is president of Royal Selangor USA and oversees the North American market. Peter Coleman, a former divisional managing director of Royal Worcester Spode, makers of fine bone china, is managing director of Royal Selangor UK. They were appointed company directors in 2002, expanding the number of board members to six.

Top: China, Malaysia and Singapore Grand Prix trophies.

Right: Veuve Clicquot Prestige champagne cooler.

Opposite: Advertisements for Plus, a range of accessories for men and women.

Others among the founder's great-grandchildren have also entered the fray.

Christopher Yong is creative consultant, coming on board after more than ten years with the UK design consultancies Addison and Citigate Lloyd Northover in Singapore and Hong Kong. Sun May Foon is a merchandiser and designer for Selberan, bringing a decade of experience gained working with Melbourne's Schlager Antique Jewellery.

■ There are other ways in which the historic enterprise has grown up. While the 1970s and 1980s were characterized by a

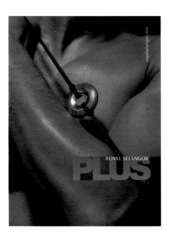

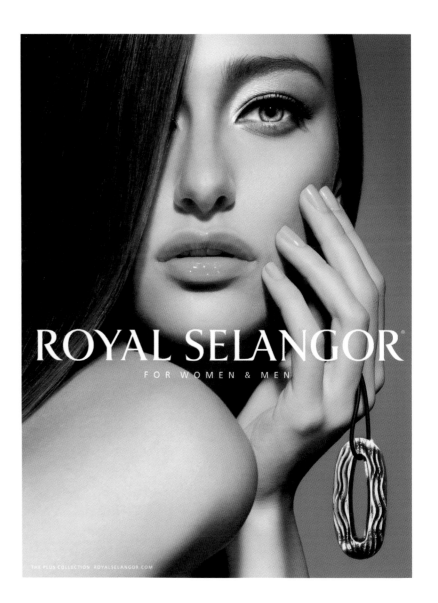

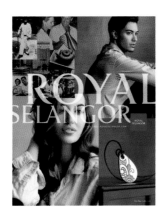

Above: A Royal Selangor advertisement, 2011.

Right: Yong Tzi Yin, a fifth generation descendant of Yong Koon, with tomorrow's heirloom, a baby mug from the Teddy Bear's Picnic range.

Below: Ladybird brooches crafted from diamonds, pearls and niobium from Selberan which won the 2001 Malaysian SIRIM award for innovation.

proliferation of retail partners around the world, the 1990s and turn of the century saw a consolidation.

The shift was a reflection of the brand's global maturity. Just as the first shop on Batu Road in the 1960s provided a venue to best showcase the pewter, the company wanted greater control over the way its products were displayed and sold internationally. That meant opening its own shops and cultivating high-end retailers.

Royal Selangor's UK experience is emblematic of the new approach to branding. In 1987, Royal Selangor bought Englefields, maker of Crown & Rose pewter. The sole remaining London pewterer was located in a former stable and its 50 employees used tools dating back to the 17th century.

Although Crown & Rose commanded a loyal following among high-end jewellers and older people, it had failed to capture the younger market. After several years of unsuccessfully trying to ride on the Crown & Rose name to penetrate the UK market, Royal Selangor hired Peter Coleman, a British giftware industry veteran.

He advocated a radical new strategy: to proudly promote the Royal Selangor brand to high-end retailers, close Englefields and move production of Crown & Rose pewter to Malaysia, re-launching the brand as Crown & Rose by Royal Selangor.

Peter cut the number of UK retail outlets, giving priority to prestigious retailers. In 1998, the company formed a retail

alliance with Arthur Price, the century-old English cutler and silversmith with two warrants from the British royal family.

In North America, the company tapped into a tradition of pewtersmithing brought by European immigrants to regions such as New England.

Royal Selangor's CY Wong remembers when he first moved to Toronto in 1988, pewter made up just a sliver of sales for the Canadian distributor William Smith, which also sells crystal and porcelain. Royal Selangor later bought William Smith and turned it into the company's base in North America. In 2002, Royal Selangor acquired Seagull Pewter, Canada's biggest pewtermaker.

Closer to home, the company stayed on the forefront of the retail scene by opening stores in top malls, including Suria KLCC, at the base of the Petronas Twin Towers, as well as visitor centres in Kuala Lumpur, Penang and Singapore. In 2011, it opened a flagship store at Pavilion Kuala Lumpur, a high-end downtown mall.

As global economic power shifts towards the east, China is now one of the company's

Image from Royal Selangor's 2011 catalogue.

115

Peter Coleman (seated), managing director of Royal Selangor UK; CY Wong, president of Royal Selangor USA.

fastest-growing markets. With department store concessions in 15 cities around China, Royal Selangor opened retail stores in Hong Kong Plaza, Shanghai in 2010 and in Guomao, Beijing in 2011.

"In key growth markets such as China, we have positioned Royal Selangor at the luxury end of the market," says Chen Tien Yue, executive director. "We believe this is the right strategy for a brand with a heritage of design and craftsmanship dating back to 1885."

More than 120 years after Yong Koon first landed on Malayan shores in a rickety Chinese junk, his legacy endures. Royal Selangor has done more than take an old-fashioned craft into the 21st century.

It has inspired a revival of interest in pewter, an ancient metal many once regarded as having limited appeal in a modern world of ceramic and glass. Inspired by this success, a host of fledgling pewter companies has emerged in the last two decades in Malaysia, Singapore, China and other parts of Asia.

Yet despite the many changes, there are traditions that remain. A central tenet is that the products must be not only beautiful but also useful.

"Our role has always been to make the products relevant to today's consumers from a functional and design viewpoint," says Yong Poh Kon. "In this way, the company and its products will continue to evolve over time." □

Royal Selangor's 125th anniversary teaset.

Company directors and grandchildren of the company's founder, (left to right) Yong Poh Kon and Yong Poh Shin standing; Sun Mun Ha (nee Yong) and Chen Mun Kuen (nee Yong) seated.

Above: Christine Lagarde, International Monetary Fund Managing Director, trying her hand at pewter hammering.

Below: 'Origins', part of the Visitor Centre's Heritage Zone.

Right: Participants of the School of Hard Knocks.

Opposite: Royal Selangor Visitor Centre.

Royal Selangor's Visitor Centre

In 2003, Royal Selangor unveiled a new visitor centre at its headquarters in Setapak Jaya, on the outskirts of Kuala Lumpur. Here, visitors from across the globe learn about the company's origins, the history of pewter in the world and the story of tin mining in Malaysia.

There is a Hall of Artefacts housing a collection of traditional tools and antique pewter from around the world.

An interactive gallery includes a Chamber of Chimes, where visitors hear the bell-like chime of cast pewter when struck, and a Hall of Finishes, where visitors run their hands along the many varieties of pewter textures to appreciate the material's malleability.

At the popular School of Hard Knocks, visitors try their hand at hammering a sheet of pewter into the shape of a bowl, as pewtersmiths did centuries ago.

The centre now attracts about 200,000 visitors a year. Buoyed by this success, Royal Selangor has opened visitor centres at Clarke Quay, Singapore and Straits Quay, Penang.

TOUCHMARKS
ASSOCIATED WITH ROYAL SELANGOR

Three immigrant brothers who sailed to Malaya from China in the 1880s started the tinsmith enterprise *Ngeok Foh*, or Jade Peace. As a sideline, the Yong brothers made ceremonial pewter items. The descendants of one brother, Yong Koon, later specialized in the pewter trade. Over the years, family feuds led to the creation of several pewter companies. The evolution of touchmarks associated with the enterprise is illustrated below:

1930–1950
Malayan Pewter Works, also known variously as Malayan Pewter, Federated Malay States (FMS) and just Malayan Pewter

1942–1963
Selangor Pewter Malaya

1979–1992
Selangor Pewter 97%

1940–1941
Tiger Pewter

1963–1965
Selangor Pewter Malaysia

ROYAL SELANGOR PEWTER

1992–2004
Royal Selangor Pewter

1945–1947
Lion Pewter

1965–1979
Selangor Pewter Malaysia - Singapore

ROYAL SELANGOR

2004
Royal Selangor

Soh Eng and Peng Kai, 1960s.

THE FAMILY TREE

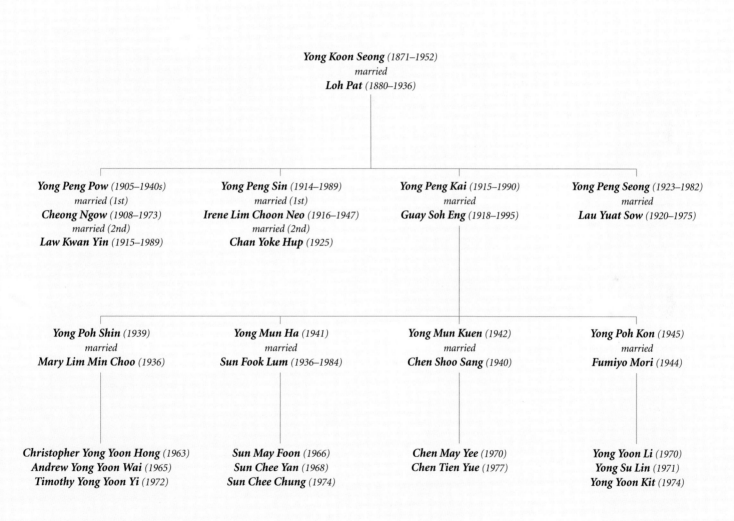

Yong Koon Seong (1871–1952)
married
Loh Pat (1880–1936)

Yong Peng Pow (1905–1940s)
married (1st)
Cheong Ngow (1908–1973)
married (2nd)
Law Kwan Yin (1915–1989)

Yong Peng Sin (1914–1989)
married (1st)
Irene Lim Choon Neo (1916–1947)
married (2nd)
Chan Yoke Hup (1925)

Yong Peng Kai (1915–1990)
married
Guay Soh Eng (1918–1995)

Yong Peng Seong (1923–1982)
married
Lau Yuat Sow (1920–1975)

Yong Poh Shin (1939)
married
Mary Lim Min Choo (1936)

Yong Mun Ha (1941)
married
Sun Fook Lum (1936–1984)

Yong Mun Kuen (1942)
married
Chen Shoo Sang (1940)

Yong Poh Kon (1945)
married
Fumiyo Mori (1944)

Christopher Yong Yoon Hong (1963)
Andrew Yong Yoon Wai (1965)
Timothy Yong Yoon Yi (1972)

Sun May Foon (1966)
Sun Chee Yan (1968)
Sun Chee Chung (1974)

Chen May Yee (1970)
Chen Tien Yue (1977)

Yong Yoon Li (1970)
Yong Su Lin (1971)
Yong Yoon Kit (1974)

TIMELINE

Yong Koon arrives in Kuala Lumpur from the Chinese port town of Shantou. He joins his two brothers who are working as tinsmiths in the tin mining town. Besides weighing scales and everyday items such as pails, they make ceremonial items for the ancestral altars of the Chinese community.

1885

1880

Kuala Lumpur's first newspaper, the English-language *Malay Mail*, prints its first edition.

1896

1900

1886

A railway line from Kuala Lumpur to Klang is completed, cutting the journey from a day's travel by river and road to 43 minutes. Tin can now be transported from Kuala Lumpur to the port in Klang four times a day.

1898

Malaya becomes the world's biggest producer of tin, with an annual output of 40,000 tonnes.

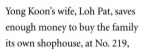

Yong Koon's wife, Loh Pat, saves enough money to buy the family its own shophouse, at No. 219, Pudu Road. The couple and their four sons – Peng Pow, Peng Sin, Peng Kai and Peng Seong – move in and start Malayan Pewter Works. After a few years, the low price of tin prompts the company to shift its focus from making Chinese ceremonial pieces to more utilitarian items, such as European-style cigarette boxes, ashtrays, vases and teapots. Loh Pat dies in 1936.

1930

The Japanese occupy Malaya, driving out the British. Peng Sin, Peng Kai and Peng Seong start Selangor Pewter. The Japanese declare tin a controlled commodity and Selangor Pewter begins making sake sets for the Japanese military. Some time during the war Peng Pow is abducted by secret society members and killed.

1942

Malayan Pewter closes.

1950

1938

1945

After a misunderstanding, Peng Pow moves out of Pudu Road and continues to operate under the name Malayan Pewter Works. In 1940 Peng Sin, Peng Kai and Peng Seong start a new company, Tiger Pewter, which closes within a year.

World War Two is over and the British return to Malaya. Peng Sin branches off and starts his own short-lived Lion Pewter. Peng Kai continues to run Selangor Pewter out of Pudu Road. He soon opens a modest retail outlet on Batu Road (now Jalan Tuanku Abdul Rahman), sharing half a shop with China Arts.

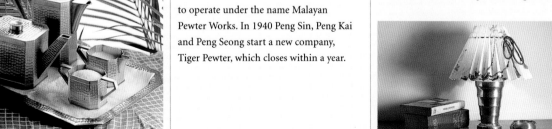

125

The patriarch Yong Koon dies at 81.

1952

Selangor Pewter moves to a modern factory in Setapak with 70 employees.

1962

Selangor Pewter opens its first full shop at No. 231, Jalan Tuanku Abdul Rahman. The shop soon becomes a popular stop for tourists to Malaysia.

1968

1957

Malaya achieves independence from the British.

One by one, Peng Kai's children join the company. Today, all four are active board directors.

1963

Malaysia is formed from the states of Malaya, Sabah and Sarawak in north Borneo, and Singapore.

Differences between the Malaysian government and the Singapore leadership result in the exit of Singapore from Malaysia in 1965.

1968

Yong Poh Shin starts a second Selangor Pewter factory in Singapore.

Selangor Pewter starts a jewellery company called Selberan, becoming one of the first Malaysian companies to design and make European-style jewellery, such as this ring in 18K gold. That same year, Selangor Pewter opens a shop at the newly-built Hilton, the best hotel in Kuala Lumpur at the time. Many more shops would follow.

1972

Selangor Pewter moves to a larger factory in Setapak with 300 employees.

1977

The husband-and-wife team of Anders Quistgaard and Guay Boon Lay set up the first formal structure for a design department, with a model room and later a wood workshop. This led to innovations such as the Admiral Line, which combined wood and pewter, and the Royal Collection, which introduced a shiny finish later used in designs by Erik Magnussen.

1978

1976

Selangor Pewter opens a shop in Hong Kong's Ocean Park. This marks the start of the company's international expansion. In the next 20 years, sales offices and shops are set up in Germany, Denmark, Japan, Australia, the UK and Canada, among others.

1979

The Sultan of Selangor confers Selangor Pewter the warrant of "Royal Pewterer."

By appointment to
HRH The Sultan of Selangor
Royal Pewterer

Selangor Pewter celebrates the centenary of Yong Koon's arrival in Malaysia with an exhibition at Muzium Negara (National Museum) in Kuala Lumpur, entitled "100 Years of Malaysian Pewter".

The company makes the world's largest pewter tankard.

1985

Yong Peng Kai dies at 75.

1990

Royal Selangor acquires London silver company Comyns, including some 35,000 historic silver designs dating back to the 17th century. The patterns cover many periods – from Rococo to Baroque to Art Nouveau.

1993

1986

The pewter exhibition moves to the National Museum Art Gallery in Singapore, under the title "Pewter in Southeast Asia".

1989

Selangor Pewter acquires Englefields, a 300-year-old London pewterer and maker of Crown & Rose pewter.

1992

Selangor Pewter is renamed Royal Selangor, reflecting its status as royal pewterer.

Royal Selangor begins a collaboration with the Victoria and Albert Museum in London. The partnership results in several ranges over the next few years under the names "The Inspired" and "William Morris".

1996

Royal Selangor opens a new visitor centre at its headquarters in Setapak Jaya, where visitors learn about the company's beginnings, the history of pewter in the world and the story of tin in Malaysia.

2003

2000

1995

Peng Kai's wife, Guay Soh Eng, dies at 78.

1998

Royal Selangor launches an interactive website, www.royalselangor.com. Customers from around the world can purchase online.

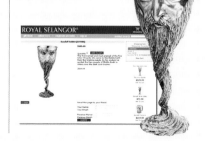

2000

ROYAL SELANGOR

Royal Selangor introduces a new namestyle and corporate identity.

2010

Royal Selangor celebrates its 125th year with the opening of a flagship store in Pavilion, a high-end shopping mall in Kuala Lumpur.

ACKNOWLEDGEMENTS

Heartfelt thanks to those who generously shared their time and memories and helped in the preparation of this book: Annie Bogermann, Peter Boorman, Chan Yoke Hup, Chen Mun Kuen (nee Yong), Chen Shoo Sang, Cho Choo Ling, Chong Hong Chong, Ivan Chong, Peter Coleman, Guay Chin Huat, Hoh Choon Tong, Hoo Wee Meng, Mohamed Jalil Haji Mohamed Daud, Keek Seng Bee, Lee Mei Hoe, Anne Leong, Gay Leong, Sharon Leong, Lim Eng, Loh Moh Yuee, Erik Magnussen, B.H. Melwani, Mistiran Haji Redwan, Julie Ng, Christopher Ponniah, Boon Lay Quistgaard (nee Guay), Salleh Haji Hassan, Janet Siew, Siti Fauziah Abdul Kadir, Sun Mun Ha (nee Yong), Sun Sai Lum, Tam Yook, Tan Huat Chye, Tan Jooi Chong, Joseph Tan, Molly Molina Tan Abdullah, Shirley Tan, Tham Tuck Hoong, Haji Wali Abdul Khalid, CY Wong, Wong Kok Nai, Wong Lai Sin, Wong Nyet Ngoh, Wong Suet Mui, Wong Wei Kim, Wong Yew Fook, Yong Fook Seong, Yong Poh Kon, Yong Poh Seong, Yong Poh Shin, Roy Yong and Amon Yuen.

Thanks to Darryl Collins, for his invaluable taped interviews with Yong Peng Kai and Yong Peng Sin in 1982, and to Katharine Yip and Ch'ng Siew Ping for acting as interpreters.

And thanks to members of my family and friends in the journalistic community for their feedback on the evolving manuscript:

Douglas Appell, Chris Beck, Chen Tien Yue, Roberto Coloma, Sonali Desai, Christine Edwards, Thomas Fuller, Jocelyn Gecker, Ling Hee Keat, Shu-Shin Luh, Raphael Pura, Sun Chee Chung, Sun Chee Yan, Sun May Foon, Pui-Wing Tam, Yong Su Lin, Yong Yoon Kit, Yong Yoon Li, Andrew Yong, Christopher Yong, Pamela Yong and Timothy Yong.

BIBLIOGRAPHY

Andaya, Barbara Watson and Andaya, Leonard Y. (2000), *A History of Malaysia*, 2nd edn, London: Palgrave.

Gullick, J.M. (2000), *A History of Kuala Lumpur* 1856–1939. MBRAS Monograph No. 29, Kuala Lumpur: Malaysian Branch of the Royal Asiatic Society.

Lee Kam Hing and Tan Chee-Beng (eds.) (2000), *The Chinese in Malaysia,* Kuala Lumpur: Oxford University Press.

Pan, Lynn (ed.), (1998), *The Encyclopedia of the Chinese Overseas,* Singapore: Archipelago Press.

Sharp, Ilsa (1985), *100 Years of Malaysian Pewter,* Kuala Lumpur: Muzium Negara, Selangor Pewter.

Shaw, William (1970), *Tin and Pewter Use.* Federation Museums Journal XV.

PICTURE CREDITS

All pictures not credited below are taken from the **Royal Selangor** archives.

Arkib Negara, p. 32, Malayan Army transport drivers; p. 36, Japanese army soldiers. **Editions Didier Millet archives**, p. 16, Masjid Jamek mosque, Yap Ah Loy; p. 18, New Government Offices; p. 19, F.M.S. poster, p. 124, F.M.S. railway line, Klang Port. **Sultan Sharafuddin Idris Shah**, p. 106 & 127, Royal Crest of Selangor; p. 111, Sultan's crown. **Shekar, S.C.**, p. 2, Chinese pewter tea caddy and antique hand tools; p. 4, *Ngeok Foh* touchmark; p. 21, Chinese wine ewer; p. 25, antique incense burner altarpiece; pp. 30–31, Yong Koon's hand tools; p. 33, pewter policeman figurine; p. 34, large pewter teapot; p. 37, whiskey measure; p. 39, Yong Koon's portrait; p. 58 & 59, 1930s pewter; p. 76, moulding handles, p. 77, soldering a vase, polishing pewter; p. 83, lapis lazuli packaging; p. 87, Sovereign Collection; p. 88, Erik Magnussen; p. 120, molten pewter; p. 125, cigarette tins. **Smith, R. J.**, p. 109, KLCC twin towers. **Timberland**, p. 110, pewter paperweights.

Illustration

Guay Boon Lay & Tan Hong Yew, p. 28, Chinese way of making pewter.

INDEX

Note: Page numbers in italic refer to illustrations.